CHINA AND
NORTHEAST ASIA

The Asia Society is a nonprofit, nonpartisan public education organization dedicated to increasing American understanding of Asia and its growing importance to the United States and to world relations. Founded in 1956, the Society covers all of Asia—30 countries from Japan to Iran and from Soviet Central Asia to the South Pacific islands. Through its programs in contemporary affairs, the fine and performing arts, and elementary and secondary education, the Society reaches audiences across the United States and works closely with colleagues in Asia.

The Contemporary Affairs department of The Asia Society seeks to . . .

- Alert Americans to the key Asian issues of the 1980s

- Illuminate the policy choices facing decision-makers in the public and private sectors

- Strengthen the dialogue between Americans and Asians on the issues and their policy implications

The department identifies issues in consultation with a group of advisers and addresses these issues through studies and publications, national and international conferences, public programs around the United States, and corporate and media activities. Major funding for the Asian Agenda program is currently provided by the Ford Foundation, the Henry Luce Foundation, the Andrew W. Mellon Foundation, Mr. and Mrs. George O'Neill, the Rockefeller Brothers Fund, and Mr. David Rockefeller.

Responsibility for the facts and opinions expressed in this publication rests exclusively with the author. His opinions and interpretations do not necessarily reflect the views of The Asia Society or its supporters.

CHINA AND NORTHEAST ASIA

THE POLITICAL DIMENSION

by Harry Harding

THE
ASIA
SOCIETY

UNIVERSITY PRESS OF AMERICA

Lanham • New York • London

Copyright © 1988 by

University Press of America,® Inc.

4720 Boston Way
Lanham, MD 20706

3 Henrietta Street
London WC2E 8LU England

Printed in the United States of America

British Cataloging in Publication Information Available

Co-published by arrangement with
The Asia Society,
725 Park Avenue, New York, New York 10021

ISBN 0–8191–6592–1 (pbk. : alk. paper)
ISBN 0–8191–6591–3 (alk. paper)

All University Press of America books are produced on acid-free
paper which exceeds the minimum standards set by the National
Historical Publications and Records Commission.

Contents

Northeast Asia

Foreword

In the years ahead Japan and the United States will face challenges to their interests and to their partnership in the Asian regional setting. How the two nations respond to changing conditions in the region will have significant consequences for other nations as well. The challenge is especially evident in Northeast Asia, where vital security interests of both nations are at stake and where economic relations are changing rapidly.

The Soviet military buildup in Northeast Asia, the confrontations on the Korean peninsula, the evolution of the Sino-Soviet relationship, and the Taiwan question make the security situation in the region one of the most sensitive and complex in the world. Political and security relations are further complicated by historic economic developments such as the opening and reform of China's economy, the emergence of Korea and Taiwan as major trading nations and competitors with Japan in some sectors, and the mounting pressure on Japan to reorient its economy. While most Americans and Japanese are focusing their attention on strains in their bilateral relationship, the potential for cooperation and conflict arising from these trends and issues has received relatively little notice. But successful management of U.S.–Japan interactions in Northeast Asia will require wider understanding in both countries.

This report is one result of a multiyear project sponsored by The Asia Society that seeks to stimulate greater American attention to U.S.–Japan interactions in Asia. The first phase of the project on "Japan, the United States and a Changing Asia" focused on Japanese and American interests and roles in Southeast Asia. It included an international conference in Japan in July 1984 that brought together more than 50 Americans, Japanese, and Southeast Asians, a report authored by Charles Morrison of the East-West Center and published in the Asian Agenda Report series, and a series of regional programs held in seven U.S. cities in February 1985.

The second phase of the project has examined the multilateral relations of Japan and the United States in Northeast Asia and has sought to stimulate wider discussion of them in the United States and between Americans and Japanese. In the fall of 1985 The Asia Society organized two study missions. The first, consisting of seven American specialists on Asian affairs, visited seven political and financial capitals of Northeast Asia to obtain the views of government officials, scholars, business people, educators, and journalists on the international relations of the region. A second study team consisting of fifteen leaders from across the United States drawn from several professional fields visited Japan for a week of briefings and discussions with Japanese officials, scholars, and journalists on Northeast Asian affairs. A conference in Japan in November 1985 brought the two American teams together with Japanese counterparts for an exchange of views on the region.

This process of international dialogue provided the basis for an array of educational outreach activities in the United States. These included lectures by the American specialists in different parts of the United States during the winter and spring of 1986, miniconferences in six American cities during May 1986 in which the American specialists and visiting Asian scholars discussed the region before diverse audiences, and a series of monographs by the American specialists on key topics relating to Japan and the United States in Northeast Asia. These monographs, including the present volume, are being published separately by The Asia Society in an Asian Agenda Report series for wide distribution around the United States and Asia.

The specialist study mission was led by Professor Robert A. Scalapino of the University of California at Berkeley, one of the United States's leading authorities on Asian affairs. The other members included distinguished scholars representing different disciplines and area specialties: Herbert Ellison, a historian of Russia and the Soviet Union who was then director of the Kennan Institute of Advanced Russian Studies in Washington, D.C. and is now at the University of Washington, Seattle; Harry Harding, a political scientist specializing on China who is senior fellow at the Brookings Institution; Donald Hellmann, a scholar of Japanese politics and foreign policy at the University of Washington, Seattle; Nicholas Lardy, a specialist on the Chinese economy who is also at the University of Washington, Seattle; Edward J. Lincoln, an economist working on Japan at the Brookings Institution; and myself (Marshall M. Bouton), representing The Asia Society.

Over a period of five weeks in October-November 1985 the Northeast Asian study mission visited Tokyo, Moscow, Ulan Bator, Beijing, Hong Kong, Taipei, and Seoul. The mission also sought to visit Pyongyang but was not granted permission to do so by the North Korean authorities. In the course of its mission the American team met with over 250 officials, scholars, journalists, and business people. This intensive schedule of discussions was made possible through the generous assistance of host organizations in all seven cities: the Japan Center for International Exchange in Tokyo; the Institute of Oriental

Studies in Moscow; the Executive Committee of the Union of Mongolian Organizations for Peace and Friendship with Other Countries in Ulan Bator, the Chinese Academy of Social Sciences in Beijing; the Universities Service Center in Hong Kong; the Institute of International Relations in Taipei; and the Asiatic Research Center of Korea University in Seoul. The Asia Society is deeply grateful for this assistance.

This report is the latest in a series produced by The Asia Society's Contemporary Affairs department as part of its national public education program, "America's Asian Agenda." The department seeks to alert Americans to critical issues in Asian affairs and in U.S.–Asian relations, to illuminate the choices which public and private policymakers face, and to strengthen transpacific dialogue on the issues. Through studies, national and international conferences, regional public programs in the United States, and corporate and media activities, the program involves American and Asian specialists and opinion-leaders in a far-reaching educational process. Asian Agenda publications emphasize short, timely reports aimed at a wide readership. Other recently published and forthcoming Asian Agenda Reports address a variety of topics including Christianity in contemporary Korea, the United States and the ANZUS alliance, financing Asian growth and development, and the Philippines and the United States.

The Asia Society wishes to acknowledge the roles played by a number of individuals and organizations in the activities leading to this report. First, the Society is deeply indebted to Robert A. Scalapino for his extraordinary leadership of the American specialist mission to Northeast Asia. His exceptional knowledge, energy, and goodwill were essential to the success of a complex and demanding endeavor. The Society is equally grateful to the other distinguished team members for their valuable contributions to the mission and other components of the project. Special thanks are also due to the leaders of the Asian organizations that arranged our programs: Tadashi Yamamoto, Evgenii Primakov, Luvsanchultem, Zhao Fusan, John Dolfin, Yu-Ming Shaw, and Han Sung-Joo. We wish also to express deep appreciation to the many individuals in the cities visited who took time from their very busy schedules to talk with the team at length.

Major financial support for the project on "Japan, the United States and a Changing Northeast Asia" has been generously provided by the United States–Japan Foundation. The Japan–United States Friendship Commission made available monies for the U.S. regional programming of the project. Critical also was funding provided for the Society's Asian Agenda program by the Ford, Rockefeller, and Henry Luce foundations and the Rockefeller Brothers Fund.

Finally, several members of the Society's staff were instrumental in the development of the project and the publications. John Bresnan assisted in the project's original overall design. Ernest Notar played an important early role in the project's phase on Northeast Asia. Most central to that second phase were Timothy J.C. O'Shea, who very ably organized all the project's activities, and Rose Wright, who provided excellent administrative assistance. Eileen D. Chang skillfully guided the publication of this and other reports emerging from the project, and Andrea Sokerka provided invaluable assistance.

Marshall M. Bouton
Director, Contemporary Affairs
The Asia Society
November 1987

Preface

If one had to choose a single region of greatest importance to Americans in terms of their livelihood, political values, and security, a leading candidate would be Northeast Asia. It is here that the most intensive economic interaction involving the United States will take place in the years immediately ahead, with interdependence—and the problems attendant to it—steadily advancing. It is here that the capacities of diverse societies to achieve and maintain a greater degree of political openness will be tested. And it is here that global and regional security issues are inextricably connected, with fateful consequences for all mankind.

In considering the future of Northeast Asia, one must juxtapose two equally important factors. On the one hand, each of the nation-states within the region bears a primary responsibility for the welfare of its own people and the strength of its domestic political and social fabric. The decisions made by the leaders of each society are especially crucial at a time when virtually every government stands at a crossroads, facing the necessity of reconsidering past economic policies, political institutions, and security strategies. Any attempt to shift the principal responsibility to external forces is fallacious.

At the same time, two nations—the United States and Japan—are deeply interrelated with both the developmental and security issues that confront the region as a whole. In their very dynamism and in the extraordinary reach of their power—economic, political, or military—they cannot avoid exerting a major influence throughout Northeast Asia. Inaction as well as action sends its message, creates an impact. Their domestic policies no less than their foreign policies have far-reaching repercussions.

It thus seemed important and timely to undertake a study of U.S. and Japanese policies in a changing Northeast Asia. In liaison with knowledgeable Japanese, we set about examining our respective roles in the region—past, present, and future.

Our task was to draw upon our background as students of Asia, supplementing this with a journey to all parts of the region available to us to hear the current ideas and proposals of Asians representing various political, economic, and national perspectives. During the course of our five-week trip, we sought first to discern those indigenous elements of a geopolitical, ideological, or economic nature that helped to shape a given society's attitudes and policies toward its neighbors, toward the region as a whole, and especially toward the

United States and Japan. We also explored the issues of greatest concern to our respondents and their views as to the appropriate remedial action. At various points, attention focused upon the question of American and Japanese policies, with an effort to examine viable alternatives as well as the potentials that existed in current policies.

On occasion, as individuals, we held different views from our Asian or Soviet friends, either with respect to the relevant data or the conclusions to be drawn from it. Being Americans, moreover, we sometimes differed among ourselves. The monograph that follows, and the others in this series, thus represent the views of the author. No effort has been made to achieve a complete consensus among us. Nevertheless, those who read all of the monographs will discover a very considerable measure of agreement on most matters of consequence.

We are enormously grateful to those individuals and organizations throughout Northeast Asia and in the Soviet Union who served as hosts, facilitators, and discussants. To exchange views in a concentrated fashion and to have the opportunity to compare and contrast the views in one society with those in another over a very short period of time proved both enlightening and stimulating.

On behalf of the group, let me also express our deep gratitude to The Asia Society and its principal officers, especially Marshall Bouton, for making possible an experience that was both enriching and enjoyable.

Robert A. Scalapino
Berkeley, California

Executive Summary

The New Era in Chinese Foreign Policy

Since the death of Mao Zedong in 1976, China has entered a new era in its foreign relations. Chinese leaders increasingly acknowledge the durability and legitimacy of the international order. They have greatly attenuated their support for revolutionary movements in the Third World and now take an increasingly active and constructive role in virtually every major international organization. In order to devote the greatest possible attention to the tasks of modernization and reform, Beijing has adopted a broad-based policy of peaceful coexistence, featuring a reduction of tensions with virtually all its former rivals and adversaries.

Relatedly, China is now engaged in unprecedently extensive foreign economic interactions in the belief that a policy of opening its economy to the outside world can accelerate the process of domestic development. It now welcomes a wide range of foreign economic relations that were proscribed during the late Maoist period, including foreign investment, foreign loans, foreign aid, and foreign advice in the management of the Chinese economy. It has also adopted an increasingly explicit separation of economics and politics so that it can establish trading relationships with countries with whom its diplomatic ties are either strained or nonexistent.

Recent years have also witnessed a growing pragmatism and flexibility in China's foreign relations. Beijing has quietly repudiated the ideological principles that were once the hallmark of its foreign policy, dealing with issues on a pragmatic, case-by-case basis. These trends reflect not only the open-mindedness of China's current leadership, but also the growing professionalization and institutionalization of the foreign policy–making process in Beijing.

Alongside these elements, however, one can also see the rise of nationalistic tendencies in Chinese foreign policy. Although Beijing still disclaims any intention to become a superpower, Chinese leaders have increasingly acknowledged their desire to build a powerful country that can play a more influential role in international affairs in the years ahead. This growing nationalism can be seen in China's adoption of an independent foreign policy and the avoidance of a close strategic alignment with either the United States or the Soviet Union. In the economic sphere, Chinese nationalism is apparent in Beijing's attempt to avoid dependence on any foreign trading partner, its desire to protect domestic industry from foreign competition, and

xiii

its insistence that China receive equal, if not preferential, treatment in international markets. On territorial matters, China continues to press border claims against many of its neighbors, and Beijing's leaders have assigned high priority to the reunification of Hong Kong, Macao, and Taiwan with the rest of the country.

China Looks at Northeast Asia

Ever since the early 1980s, China has adopted a considerably more flexible and conciliatory posture toward the Soviet Union than it had in the 1970s. Thus far, however, the most dramatic improvements in Sino-Soviet relations have been limited to the economic and cultural spheres. The Chinese still insist that the full normalization of political relations with the Soviet Union can occur only if there is progress toward removing what it describes as the "three obstacles" to the development of Sino-Soviet relations: the stationing of "massive armed forces" along the Sino-Soviet and Sino-Mongolian frontiers; the Soviet Union's intervention in Afghanistan; and Moscow's support for Vietnam's "invasion and occupation" of Cambodia, on which Chinese leaders now place particular emphasis.

Although there may well be some further progress in Sino-Soviet relations in the years ahead, there will also be limits on how far Beijing will move toward a true accommodation with the Soviet Union. China's desire for an independent foreign policy precludes a return to the kind of alliance with the Soviet Union that existed in the 1950s. Chinese leaders would not want to sacrifice their growing economic and military cooperation with the United States for the sake of a reduction of tensions with the Soviet Union. Nor are there any indications that China has altered its underlying perception that the Soviet Union remains the principal threat to its national security.

The last decade has also seen a rapid development of Sino-Japanese relations, in both the political and economic spheres. China now conducts approximately one-quarter of its foreign trade with Japan, with Chinese imports of Japanese equipment financed in part by Japanese loans and export credits.

Even so, Sino-Japanese relations remain somewhat fragile. The mistrust created by 50 years of military confrontation and reinforced by another quarter century of political isolation cannot easily be removed. From the Chinese perspective, four problems loom large in assessing their relations with Japan. Perhaps the most emotional issue is the possible resurgence of Japanese militarism, as symbolized by the recent Japanese decision to increase its defense spending above the long-standing limit of one percent of GNP. Other irritants in Sino-Japanese relations include the chronic imbalances in Sino-Japanese trade, the continued economic and political relations between Japan and Taiwan, and the territorial disputes over a small group of islands located just northeast of Taiwan. By early 1987 these issues had combined to create the highest level of tension between two countries since the signing of their treaty of peace and friendship in 1978.

Recent years have revealed that China differs with North Korea over several key issues. It has a distaste for the unreformed Stalinism of Kim Il-sung and has attempted to persuade the North Korean leadership to consider a course of political liberalization and economic reform. Beijing has a stronger interest than Pyongyang in maintaining peace and stability on the Korean peninsula. Moreover, despite Pyongyang's objections, China has shown a determination to establish and maintain unofficial contacts with South Korea. Partly out of irritation with China, North Korea has engaged in a significant improvement of its relations with Moscow, including an expansion of its military ties with the Soviet Union.

Still, despite these differences in perspective, China has sought to avoid any deterioration in its relations with Pyongyang. Beijing realizes that strong ties with North Korea are essential if China is to be able to dissuade it from attacking the South or from forging a close alignment with the Soviet Union. China has accordingly maintained a constant stream of high-level visitors to and from North Korea, supplied Pyongyang with relatively sophisticated military equipment, supported most of North Korea's diplomatic initiatives toward the United States and the South, and periodically cut back its economic ties with Seoul when confronted with strong objections from North Korea. The PRC has also urged the United States to adopt a more flexible policy toward North Korea.

A final element in China's relations with Northeast Asia involves the three territories which Beijing hopes to reincorporate into China by the end of the century: Macao, Hong Kong, and Taiwan. In 1984, after long and difficult negotiations, China and Great Britain reached an agreement over the future of Hong Kong. It provided that Hong Kong would become a "special administrative region" of China in 1997, with a "high degree of autonomy" in most matters and with its present social and economic order basically intact. The terms of the agreement—which was more binding and more forthcoming than most observers had believed possible—reflect Beijing's interest in preserving Hong Kong's stability and prosperity after its return to Chinese sovereignty. Still, China appears reluctant to agree to any significant degree of political liberalization in Hong Kong for fear that democracy would create social and economic instability in the territory and might dilute its own control over developments there.

Beijing would also like to apply the concept of "one country, two systems" to Taiwan and has indicated that it would interpret the formula even more flexibly there than in Hong Kong. China has also reiterated its preference for a peaceful solution to the Taiwan question. Even so, the PRC continues to rule out any solution that would not acknowledge Taiwan as a local jurisdiction of the People's Republic of China and adamantly refuses to rule out the use of force against the island. Moreover, it can be expected to react quickly and sharply to the emergence of a strong Taiwan independence movement or to any signs that either Japan or the United States is retreating from past commitments on the Taiwan question.

Northeast Asia Looks at China

The countries of Northeast Asia regard contemporary China with considerable ambivalence. Most of them are pleased with the main features of Beijing's present foreign policy, particularly its emphasis on economic modernization, its desire for a peaceful international environment, its growing pragmatism and flexibility, and its increasing support for the international political and economic order. But over the longer term, China's modernization means that Beijing will have greater material resources with which to pursue its international objectives, and growing Chinese nationalism raises the possibility that those goals may be defined in ways that compete or conflict with the interests of other Asian states.

The two largest powers in the region, Japan and the Soviet Union, are reasonably sanguine about their relations with China, both now and for the immediate future. Over the longer run, however, many Soviet and Japanese analysts share a common concern that Beijing's program of economic modernization will transform China into a powerful, assertive, and disruptive military and political force in Asia. In Japan, there also persists a sizable body of opinion that China's effort at economic reform will ultimately fail and that the PRC will descend into social and political disorder. In either scenario, China would come to have a profoundly destabilizing influence on the rest of the region.

In contrast, the perceptions of China in both halves of the Korean peninsula are among the most favorable in Asia. Each of the two Koreas sees Beijing as a potential source of support in its struggle against its rival. Pyongyang can point to its alliance with Beijing, while Seoul can find evidence that China serves as a restraint against North Korean adventurism. Neither country regards China as a direct threat to its own security.

But neither Korea can be absolutely certain that Beijing will, in the final analysis, remain completely reliable. Seoul fears that China's past commitments to North Korea, together with its continuing rivalry with the Soviet Union for influence in Pyongyang, would force Beijing to choose the North over the South in any crisis on the Korean peninsula. Similarly, Pyongyang probably regards Beijing's flirtation with Seoul as clear evidence of Chinese infidelity and may assume that China's growing ties with the United States would prevent it from giving wholehearted support to the North in the event of renewed hostilities along the Demilitarized Zone (DMZ).

The three remaining parts of Northeast Asia—Hong Kong, Taiwan, and Mongolia—express the greatest anxiety about China's long-term intentions and capabilities, for each of them perceives itself to be a target of Chinese irredentism. Still, there is also a modicum of hope in each place that China will act with flexibility and restraint in the years ahead.

In Hong Kong, there is now a general consensus that Beijing genuinely wishes to maintain economic prosperity and social stability in the territory before and after its return to Chinese sovereignty. But there is not yet complete confidence that China will provide adequate legal guarantees of Hong Kong's autonomy or will permit the creation of a sufficiently responsive and democratic system of local government.

Many older Nationalist officials on Taiwan maintain an unyielding posture toward Beijing, opposing either negotiation, contact, or compromise with the PRC. But some younger people on the island, both inside and outside the Kuomintang, are more supportive of a relaxation of tensions and the opening of unofficial contacts between Taiwan and the mainland. In response to these pressures, the Taiwan government has recently tolerated a higher level of indirect trade with the mainland, sanctioned academic contacts with mainland scholars in third countries, and agreed to participate in nonofficial international organizations alongside Beijing.

Despite repeated Chinese protestations to the contrary, Mongolia appears convinced that Beijing would like to absorb it into Chinese territory. As a result, Ulan Bator has turned to Moscow for military support, accepting in return a high degree of economic integration with the Soviet Union. Nonetheless, as a result of Gorbachev's decision in July 1986 to withdraw a part of Soviet forces from

Mongolia, Ulan Bator has sought to improve its relations with Beijing somewhat and has established diplomatic relations with the United States, while simultaneously exploring the possibility of expanding its economic relations with Japan.

Implications for the United States and Japan

Through the rest of the century, Beijing is likely to continue to assign the highest priority to economic development and reform and, therefore, to seek a peaceful international environment. At the same time, China will remain concerned about its national security and will view the Soviet Union as its principal strategic rival. Increasingly, however, it will also view with apprehension the rise of Japanese military power. Third, Beijing will continue to place considerable emphasis on national reunification, although its policies toward Hong Kong, Macao, and Taiwan are likely to remain flexible and pragmatic. And finally, as its modernization proceeds, China's economic power, political influence, and military strength are all likely to increase. It is unlikely that China will use these resources to support an aggressive or expansionist policy, but Beijing will use its growing power to ensure its participation in the solution of regional issues and to gain access to the foreign markets, capital, and technology it needs for development.

These developments imply that, in the years ahead, the United States and China will share common interests on some subjects but hold divergent perspectives on others, much as they do today. On balance, however, the commonalities should continue to outweigh the differences. This important fact will make it increasingly possible for the two countries to act in parallel or collaborative fashion on those issues in which they have similar objectives and to manage their remaining differences in a mature and responsible manner. If this can be done, then Sino-American relations may well enter a new stage, featuring growing trust and cooperation.

I. Introduction

More than 150 years ago, surveying the strategic environment of his day, Napoleon Bonaparte looked east toward China. He saw a nation that, despite its rich history, was encumbered by technological inferiority, economic stagnation, and political decay. Nonetheless, Napoleon was disturbed by China's potential. "There lies China," he is said to have warned. "Let her sleep. For when she wakes, she will shake the world."

China is now awakening. Its vast human and material resources are, in the post-Mao era, being mobilized by policies that offer the hope of more rapid, effective, and sustained economic growth than the country has ever experienced before. Its large but cumbersome military establishment is being streamlined, reorganized, and re-equipped, with the promise of becoming a smaller but more efficient armed force. China is engaged more actively in international economic and diplomatic relations than at any other time in its history.

Northeast Asia—defined here as including Japan, North and South Korea, the Soviet Union, Mongolia, Taiwan, and Hong Kong—is naturally a central focus of China's reawakening. At the beginning of the 1980s Deng Xiaoping, China's preeminent leader, set forth three overarching policy objectives that China would pursue for the rest of the decade and beyond: preserving national security, pursuing economic modernization, and achieving national reunification. Northeast Asia plays a vital role with regard to each of these three policy goals. The principal threats to Chinese national security come from the long, disputed Sino-Soviet and Sino-Mongolian borders, as well as from the volatile situation on the Korean peninsula. Northeast Asia is home to China's largest trading partners, Japan and Hong Kong, and to several smaller economies, including South Korea and Taiwan, which Beijing believes can provide valuable lessons about development strategy. National reunification, in the present context, refers primarily to the process of reasserting Beijing's sovereignty over Taiwan, Hong Kong, and Macao.

This is not to say that Northeast Asia is the sole arena of Chinese foreign policy. As a large continental power, China also has important security interests to the south and west. Beijing today is as concerned with Soviet activities in Afghanistan and the Vietnamese invasion of Cambodia as it is with the buildup of Soviet forces in Siberia and Mongolia. It still has a potentially serious border dispute with India. And as a regional power with global aspirations, China

1

devotes considerable attention to developments in the Soviet-American rivalry in the Middle East, Africa, and Latin America as well as in Asia. On the economic dimension, China looks to Eastern Europe as well as to the smaller newly industrializing countries (NICs) of East Asia for strategies of economic development and structural reform. And it seeks capital, technology, and markets in Western Europe and the United States as well as in Japan.

Nonetheless, no region of the world is more important to China than is Northeast Asia. And, in turn, given its proximity to China, no region of the world will be more deeply affected by China's re-awakening than Northeast Asia.

Although it is highly likely that China will continue to modernize socially, economically, and militarily for the rest of this century, it is less clear whether the second half of the Napoleonic prophecy will be vindicated. Thus far, in fact, the main trend in Chinese foreign policy in the post-Mao era has been toward stabilization rather than disruption. China's overwhelming concern with its economic development leads Beijing to seek a peaceful international environment and to forge economic linkages with virtually every conceivable trading partner. It has also produced greater flexibility and pragmatism in Chinese foreign policy and a reduction of tensions with many countries that were once China's adversaries.

Nonetheless, looking toward the future, there are other aspects of Chinese foreign policy that may someday be cause for disquiet. One is the rise of nationalism in China, as the grip of ideology over Chinese society gradually weakens. Nationalism is reflected in the continuing mistrust of the foreign economic and cultural presence in China, in the desire for economic and strategic independence from stronger powers, in the insistence on reunifying China on Beijing's terms, and even in some assertions of China's right to a leadership role in Asia. When coupled with the projected growth of China's military and economic strength, the emergence of nationalism in China is understandably of considerable concern to China's neighbors in Northeast Asia. Clearly, the region faces the need to accommodate a new major power—a process which is rarely easy and can sometimes be disastrous.

Thus, when the Northeast Asian states look at China, they do so with some ambivalence. Generally speaking, they are pleased by the immediate results of China's current concentration on economic modernization and reform but worry about the long-term consequences if that process proves successful. The particular blend of optimism and concern varies, however, from one capital to another. The two Koreas are the most sanguine about China, for they see it as

2

a friendly nation and as a potential counterweight to nations they regard as more serious threats. The two major regional powers—Japan and the Soviet Union—benefit from the best relations they have had with China in years and forecast further improvements in their ties with Beijing, but both privately express concern about China's growing military strength. At the far end of the spectrum of anxiety, Hong Kong, Macao, Taiwan, and Mongolia all fear the prospect of absorption by a more powerful China.

The rise of China poses both challenges and opportunities for American policies toward Northeast Asia. The principal strategic issue in the region concerns, as it has for 40 years, the triangular relationship between China, the United States, and the Soviet Union. In the 1950s, China entered an alliance with the Soviet Union against the United States; some twenty years later, it appeared to welcome a united front with the United States against the Soviet Union. Today, China has proclaimed an independent foreign policy and has foresworn any alliance with either superpower against the other. How does this development affect American interests? What kind of strategic relationship can now be forged between Beijing and Washington? And how should the United States react to the recent gradual reduction of tensions between China and the Soviet Union?

Second, Sino-American relations are a critical element in the successful management of the two most potentially explosive regions in Northeast Asia—Korea and Taiwan. Both Beijing and Washington now share a desire to maintain stability on the Korean peninsula and in the Taiwan Strait. But China retains a formal military alliance with North Korea and is committed to the reunification of Taiwan with the mainland. This complex situation suggests both risks and benefits for the United States. How can Washington most effectively enlist China in the effort to maintain security on the Korean peninsula while reinforcing its preference for a peaceful future for Taiwan? What policy should the United States adopt toward the sale of American arms to Taiwan? How should it respond to the competing calls of the Chinese government for the reunification of China with those of some quarters in Taiwan for the self-determination of the people of the island?

Finally, there is in Northeast Asia an emerging triangular relationship linking China, the United States, and Japan. For the first time, all of these countries are friendly toward each other. Still, there are differences in perception among them that could complicate their relationships. Both Tokyo and Beijing are apprehensive of each other's programs of military modernization, suggesting that the United States should develop strategic links with both countries

3

gradually and prudently. If Taiwan were to become an active issue in either Sino-American or Sino-Japanese relations the result could conceivably be a deterioration in Japanese-American ties as well. Finally, there remains the possibility of a strain between Japan and the United States resulting from the pace at which economic ties with China are expanded, particularly if the Japanese are believed to be using unfair practices to gain economic advantage. None of these issues is likely to create an actual crisis, but the potential differences of interest and perception must be carefully monitored and addressed if relations among the three countries are to remain stable.

II. The New Era
in Chinese Foreign Policy

China's relations with Northeast Asia are almost as old as Chinese civilization itself. China's contacts with Korea date to the first century B.C., and direct connections with Japan were established in the following century. From a broad historical perspective, these two thousand years of linkages between China and its Northeast Asian neighbors can be divided into four periods.

During the first and longest period, from the Qin and Han dynasties in the third century B.C. to the late Qing dynasty in the nineteenth century A.D., China regarded itself as the "middle kingdom," the *center* of all of East Asia. By turns cosmopolitan and isolationist, unified and divided, vibrant and stagnant, throughout this period China was the most important cultural, economic, and political force in the region.

In the second period, which extended roughly from 1800 to 1950, China saw itself as the *victim* of an expanding Western imperial order. First the Russians, then the British, then the French and the Germans, and finally the Japanese and the Americans came to China to seek profit, influence, and territory. Weakened by economic decline, political decay, and technological backwardness, China was unable to resist these encroachments until the Communist Party created a powerful new central government on the mainland in 1949, which was committed to expelling unwanted foreign influence.

The years from 1950 through the death of Mao Zedong in 1976 represent a third period in China's foreign relations. In this quarter century of Maoist rule, a revolutionary China regarded itself as the *challenger* of the postwar international economic and political order that centered on the United States. At first, Beijing waged this struggle in alliance with the Soviet Union; then, from 1960 on, it did so in concert with radical movements and regimes elsewhere in the Third World. The hallmark of this period was China's isolation from established international organizations and from the mainstream of the world economy—an isolation that was partly self-imposed and partly forced upon Beijing by the United States.

Since 1976 China has entered a new era in its foreign relations. China has become an active *participant* in the same postwar system that it had sought to overthrow in the 1950s and 1960s. It has joined virtually every major intergovernmental organization, from the International Monetary Fund to the International Atomic Energy Agency;

5

it has greatly increased the volume of its trade with foreign countries; and it has vastly expanded the range of its foreign economic relationships. In large part, this transformation reflects the Sino-American rapprochement of the 1970s, which was based in turn on the common perception of a strategic threat from the Soviet Union. In addition, the new era in Beijing's foreign relations has also resulted from the change in China's domestic priorities, from continuous revolution under Mao to economic modernization and reform under Deng Xiaoping.

Three Earlier Periods in China's Foreign Relations

In traditional times, the main pattern in China's foreign relations was the interaction of a relatively advanced Chinese agrarian culture with less sophisticated nomadic peoples on China's periphery. One of the principal features of this earliest period in China's foreign relations was the attempt to maintain its security in the face of invasions from the north and northeast. The Great Wall of China, the construction of which was completed during the Qin dynasty, was a symbol of China's efforts to keep the northern tribes at bay. So too were the efforts by the Ming dynasty to defend Korea against Japanese encroachment and to guard the Chinese coast against Japanese pirates, and the military campaign by both the Ming and the Qing to subdue the Mongols.

The attempts to pacify the northern borders were not always successful. On several occasions, particularly when China itself had been weakened by economic decline or political decay, nomadic tribes were able to establish their own rule over parts of northern China, or even over the entire Chinese empire. These foreign dynasties from the north include not only the Yuan (the Mongol dynasty, which ruled from 1279 to 1368) and the Qing (the Manchu dynasty, which governed China between 1644 and 1912), but also lesser kingdoms such as the Liao (916–1125) and the Jin (1115–1234), which controlled parts of northern China.

And yet, the nomadic invaders were usually attracted by the superiority of Chinese culture, and their dynasties gradually became an amalgam of their own traditions and those of China. The sinicization of foreign rulers reflects a second broad feature of the foreign relations of traditional China: the extension of China's cultural and political influence over many parts of Northeast Asia. The influence of China was greatest in Korea, which was a tributary state of China for most of the period from the Tang dynasty to modern times. The

6

influence of Chinese art, religion, architecture, language, and philosophy is also apparent in Japan, even though Japan accepted Chinese suzerainty much more sporadically and superficially. The Chinese legacy is less evident in Mongolia, where the Gobi desert and a strong Buddhist tradition served as effective physical and cultural barriers to Chinese ideas and values.

During the early modern period, from around 1600 to 1949, the military and technological balance between China and the foreigners gradually began to change, ushering in a second stage in China's international relations. The rise of the West, and later the modernization of Japan, brought China into contact, for the first time in its history, with foreign societies that were arguably more advanced than China itself. Moreover, these foreigners sought to gain access to China for trade, missionary work, and ultimately territorial acquisition. By the end of the eighteenth century, too, China itself had been weakened by population pressures, economic stagnation, and political corruption and had entered a period of protracted dynastic decline. The conjunction of these two developments—the decay of China and the rise of Europe and Japan—had a devastating impact on China.

Initially, the demands of the Europeans were limited and could be handled in the same ways China had dealt with foreign nomads in the past. Foreigners were allowed limited access to Beijing; a small number of coastal ports and border crossings were open to foreign trade; and China's boundaries with its neighbors were more clearly demarcated. Thus, in 1686 Qing China and tsarist Russia signed the Treaty of Nerchinsk, which delineated the Manchurian portion of the frontier between the two empires and established a more stable basis for Sino-Russian trade. Somewhat less than 50 years later, a further agreement allowed Russia to send trade caravans to Beijing every three years and to establish a Russian Orthodox church and a language school in the Chinese capital. Similar arrangements allowed Western European nations limited access to trade along China's southeastern coast.

Gradually, however, the rapidly modernizing European nations became dissatisfied with these arrangements, and their increasing technological advantage gave them the military means with which they could compel China to alter them. During the first half of the nineteenth century, the European objective was to force China open for commercial activities and missionary work and to establish small enclaves in a growing number of coastal cities. By the end of the century, however, the territorial ambitions of the Europeans became more extensive. Entire ports were ceded or leased to European

7

powers, including Hong Kong and Weihaiwei to Britain, Qingdao to Germany, Macao to Portugal, Guangzhouwan to France, and Dalian to Russia. Large parts of China were claimed by foreign powers as their exclusive spheres of influence. To the north, tsarist Russia attempted to establish such spheres of influence in both Manchuria and Xinjiang. It was also able to acquire the Maritime Province surrounding Vladivostok in 1860 and to secure Outer Mongolia's independence from China in 1911.

Particularly galling to China was the successful participation of Japan, its former vassal state, in the process of gaining political, economic, and territorial advantages in China. By the end of the nineteenth century Japan had begun to follow the same policies as the European powers, winning extraterritorial privileges in China, wresting peripheral territories (such as Korea and Taiwan) from Chinese rule, acquiring treaty ports along the Chinese coast, and competing with Russia for a sphere of influence in Manchuria. As China weakened further after the revolution of 1911, Japanese demands increased. By the late 1920s Tokyo had begun to create a series of puppet states inside northern China, and in 1937 Japan launched an all-out invasion of the country.

The establishment of the People's Republic in 1949—which ended 150 years of rebellion and revolution in China—marked the beginning of the third stage in China's foreign relations. Angered and humiliated by their country's treatment at the hands of Japan and the West, the leaders of the young Communist regime were committed to restoring national unity, protecting territorial integrity, modernizing their economy, and regaining a degree of international influence and prestige. For a time during World War II, Mao Zedong and Zhou Enlai had hoped that the United States would prove to be a more progressive sort of industrial power than the European or Japanese imperialists had been and that the Chinese Communist movement would receive American moral and material support. By the late 1940s, however, they had concluded that the Americans, now the dominant force in the postwar international system, were not fundamentally different from the British or the Germans before them. In Mao's words, the Chinese people would have to "cast away illusions" and "prepare for struggle" with the United States. The Chinese Communist Party now portrayed itself as one of the principal challengers of the prevailing international order.

At first, China's new revolutionary leadership believed that a close relationship with the Soviet Union would be the best strategy for pursuing its goals, particularly given the common ideological commitments of the two countries. Gradually, however, friction between

8

Moscow and Beijing wore away at the Sino-Soviet alliance. Beijing became convinced that the Kremlin was attempting to exercise political and economic control over China, that it would sacrifice Chinese interests in its own dealings with the United States, and that it was exporting to China a model of economic development that was unsuited to Chinese needs. Moreover, territorial disputes left over from earlier periods—the traditional Russian interests in Manchuria and Xinjiang and disagreements over the location of the border in both these regions—contributed to the deterioration of Sino-Soviet relations. By 1956 the Sino-Soviet alliance was fraying; by 1960, it had virtually collapsed.

Throughout the 1960s and much of the 1970s, therefore, China attempted to take on both superpowers simultaneously, aligning itself with what it regarded as "progressive" elements in the Third World. At times, such as during the mid-1960s, Beijing defined this category extremely narrowly, associating itself with a handful of radical regimes, Communist insurgencies, and national liberation movements that had sufficiently revolutionary orientations. In other periods, such as during the early 1970s, China advocated the creation of a broader "united front" of established Third World governments that would fight against the hegemonism of the two superpowers and struggle for the restructuring of the international economic order. But these variations notwithstanding, the common denominator was China's continued challenge to the prevailing international system, which it now declared was dominated by both the United States and the Soviet Union to the detriment of smaller and weaker states.

Although Beijing continued to regard the United States as an imperialist power, its relations with Washington underwent a gradual evolution after the Korean War. Despite their mutual hostility, after the Korean armistice the two sides reached a common understanding of the desirability of avoiding any further direct military confrontation. Beginning in 1955, therefore, China and the United States maintained a fairly regular diplomatic dialogue at the ambassadorial level, first in Geneva and then in Warsaw. These contacts enabled them to manage and defuse the periodic crises that erupted over the small islands along the Chinese coast that were still held by the Nationalist government on Taiwan.

By the late 1960s increasing Sino-Soviet tensions had convinced Beijing that its principal adversary was not the United States but the Soviet Union. At the same time, the United States, bogged down in a protracted conflict in Vietnam, was eager for a bold diplomatic initiative that might increase its leverage over both Hanoi and Moscow. As a result, Beijing and Washington moved rapidly toward a mutual rapprochement in the early 1970s, as symbolized by Henry Kissinger's secret visit to Beijing in 1971 and Richard Nixon's subsequent trip the following spring. At this point, the principal factor moving the two countries toward a more normal relationship was their common concern about Soviet expansion in East Asia. Indeed, by the end of the 1970s Chinese leaders had begun to talk about a "united front" with the United States against the Soviet Union, and American officials described China as a partner in a quasi-alliance. Increasingly, however, the improvement of Sino-American relations was reinforced by economic considerations as, even in the late Maoist period, China began to look abroad for the advanced technology it needed to accelerate its economic development.

China's relations with the smaller Communist nations of Northeast Asia—North Korea and Mongolia—were shaped during the Maoist era by the evolution of China's ties with the Soviet Union. When Beijing's alliance with Moscow was strong, its relations with Pyongyang and Ulan Bator were also relatively untroubled. But as the Sino-Soviet relationship deteriorated, the two smaller Communist countries were caught in the middle. They chose two different courses. Mongolia, out of its fear of Chinese irredentism, maintained a firm alliance with the Soviet Union and, after 1966, accepted the deployment of a substantial number of Soviet air and ground forces inside its territory. North Korea, perceiving less threat from the PRC, opted for a more balanced policy, preserving reasonably cordial relations with both Moscow and Beijing, but tilting noticeably toward China. The turmoil of the Cultural Revolution briefly disrupted Beijing's friendly ties to Pyongyang, but the damage done by the Red Guard movement was quickly repaired.

Conversely, China's policy toward Japan and South Korea was strongly influenced by Beijing's relations with the United States. During the 1950s and 1960s, with Sino-American tensions at their height, China maintained no relations whatsoever with South Korea, which it regarded as little more than a puppet of the United States. During the same period, while criticizing the Japanese government for its military alliance with the United States and for its continuing diplomatic relations with Taiwan, China also sought to cultivate economic and political ties with sympathetic groups and individuals inside Japan, in the hope of luring Japan away from the anti-Chinese economic embargo and military alliance created by the United States. When Sino-American relations started to improve in the 1970s, Chinese attitudes toward South Korea and Japan also began to change. Within seven months after the Nixon visit to China in 1972 Beijing and Tokyo had normalized their diplomatic relations, and

China began expressing support for the Japanese-American alliance. By the end of the decade, China was also exploring the possibility of limited economic links to South Korea.

This third stage in China's foreign relations also witnessed periodic efforts to promote the reunification of Taiwan with the mainland, sometimes through the use of force against the offshore islands held by the Nationalists, and sometimes through political overtures to the Kuomintang or the United States. A key element in either strategy was to create strains in the relationship between the United States and Taiwan, either by creating doubts in Washington over the wisdom of its alliance with the Nationalists, or by raising questions in Taipei about the long-term durability of the American commitment. Beijing's rapprochement with the United States in the 1970s represented a major breakthrough in this strategy, even though it did not lead to any immediate signs that Taipei was prepared to consider reunification with the mainland. Interestingly, Beijing devoted much less attention to its other irredentist claims to Hong Kong and Macao, apparently believing that the time was not yet ripe to challenge British and Portuguese rule over those small territories.

China's Foreign Relations under Deng Xiaoping

Since the death of Mao Zedong in 1976 and the rise of Deng Xiaoping in subsequent years, China's domestic policy has moved in dramatically new directions. Economic modernization has been given the highest priority on the national agenda, with the Maoist interest in maintaining the purity of the revolutionary vision now virtually extinct. Moreover, economic development is being pursued through policies that mark a drastic departure from the Maoist and Stalinist models of the past. Society has been granted more autonomy from the state, the economy more autonomy from the plan, the government more autonomy from the Party, and intellectual and cultural life more autonomy from ideology.

The new course in China's domestic affairs has been strongly reinforced by changes in the international environment. In Chinese eyes, the military competition between the two superpowers has reached a new and relatively stable equilibrium. No longer is there the danger, as in the 1950s, that the United States would establish dominance over the Soviet Union, or conversely, as in the 1970s, that the Soviet Union might gain a permanent advantage over the United States. Because of this new balance, and because of the restoration of political stability inside China after the turmoil of the Cultural

11

Revolution, China can now be more relaxed about its national security than at any time since 1949.

At the same time, China can also take comfort in the fact that its standing in the international system is higher than at any time since the end of the eighteenth century. No longer is China regarded as the "sick man of Asia" and the object of invasion or exploitation by foreign powers, as it was in the nineteenth and early twentieth centuries. No longer is Beijing isolated from the mainstream of the international community, as it was because of American policy in the 1950s and then by its own choice in the 1960s. Today, Beijing has secured the formal recognition of all major nations, occupies a permanent seat on the United Nations Security Council, is respected as a major regional power in East Asia, and is considered by some analysts to be a "candidate superpower" which will make an increasing mark on global issues as well.

If the international strategic environment is somewhat more pacific, the regional economic environment is more challenging to China. As China emerged from the Cultural Revolution, it realized that it had been surpassed economically not only by Japan but also by the smaller newly industrialized countries of East Asia, including South Korea, Hong Kong, and Taiwan. Beijing's awareness of the intensifying economic competition in the region reinforced its decision to assign highest priority to the task of economic modernization, and also produced considerable interest in learning more about the reasons for the economic success of its Northeast Asian neighbors.

These domestic and international developments have had several significant implications for Chinese foreign relations in the post-Mao era. To begin with, now that their standing in the international order has increased, Chinese leaders increasingly acknowledge the durability and legitimacy of that system. In more revolutionary days, China called at various times for widespread people's war against the two superpowers, disparaged the United Nations and other international organizations, gave moral and material support to radical movements overseas, and proposed the creation of a new international economic order. Today, such revolutionary rhetoric has virtually disappeared from Chinese statements about international affairs. China has greatly attenuated, although not completely eliminated, even its moral support for revolutionary movements in the Third World. Beijing has joined virtually every international organization and takes an increasingly active and constructive role in their work. Although China continues to envision changes in the international economic system, its statements on the subject call for negotiation

12

and compromise rather than confrontation between the developed and the developing nations.

Second, Beijing is interested in ensuring a peaceful international environment, particularly in East Asia, so as to be able to devote the greatest possible energies to the tasks of modernization and reform. China has adopted what might be called a policy of "omnidirectional peaceful coexistence," featuring a reduction of tensions with virtually all of its former rivals and adversaries, with the single glaring exception of Vietnam. Beijing actively discourages the resumption of hostilities on the Korean peninsula and appears to favor détente between the Soviet Union and the United States. Although engaged in a gradual program of military modernization, China has given its armed forces a relatively low priority when determining the national budget. In sharp contrast to the Maoist era, when Beijing insisted that either world war or world revolution was inevitable, China now has concluded that the prospects for world peace and stability are excellent.

Third, China is now engaged in unprecedentedly extensive foreign economic interactions, in the belief that a policy of opening to the outside world can greatly accelerate the process of economic modernization and reform. Beijing has increased its foreign trade, measured as a proportion of its gross national product, to the highest level since 1949. It now welcomes a wide range of foreign economic relations that were proscribed during the latter Maoist period, including foreign investment, foreign loans, foreign aid, and foreign advice in the management of the Chinese economy. Moreover, like Japan in the 1960s, Beijing today has engaged in an increasingly explicit separation of economics and politics so that it can establish trading relationships with countries, such as South Korea, with whom its diplomatic ties are either strained or nonexistent.

Fourth, recent years have witnessed a growing pragmatism and flexibility in China's foreign relations. Although the repudiation of past ideological premises has not been as thoroughgoing in international relations as in domestic affairs, Beijing has quietly abandoned the doctrinalism that was once the hallmark of its foreign policy. Instead, China increasingly deals with issues on a pragmatic, case-by-case basis, with explicit reference to China's national interest. As Premier Zhao Ziyang put it in 1986, Beijing will establish its position on international issues "on the merits of each case" and will not determine its "closeness with or estrangement from other countries on the basis of their social systems and ideologies."[1] This new

---

[1]"Report on the Seventh Five-Year Plan," *Beijing Review*, April 21, 1986, p. xviii.

pragmatism has enabled Beijing to be more flexible and less rigid than in the past in its treatment of major international issues. These trends reflect not only the openmindedness of China's current leadership, but also the growing professionalization and institutionalization of the foreign policy–making process in Beijing.

Alongside these developments one can also see the rise of nationalistic tendencies in Chinese foreign policy. Although Beijing still disclaims any intention to become a "superpower"—if only because that term carries with it a decidedly pejorative connotation in Chinese eyes—Chinese leaders have been increasingly outspoken in their acknowledgment that one of the purposes of their current program of economic modernization is to build a powerful China that will play an even more influential role in international affairs in the years to come. As Deng Xiaoping pointed out in October 1984, by the year 2000 China will be able to have an annual military budget of some $50 billion by allocating merely five percent of its gross national product to national defense. By that time, Deng said, "China will be truly powerful, exerting a much greater influence in the world."[2]

A revived Chinese nationalism is evident among ordinary Chinese as well as among their leaders. There have been spontaneous popular demonstrations after international sporting events, which have carried a patriotic flavor when the Chinese team has won but have had xenophobic overtones when China has lost. At the end of 1985 there was a wave of student protests in a number of Chinese cities, criticizing among other issues the alleged revival of militarism in Japan and the growing Japanese economic presence in China. The visit of a small American flotilla to Qingdao—the first port call by the U.S. Navy since 1949—occasioned a small anti-American protest by students from the local maritime academy. And young intellectuals have echoed their leaders' calls for a more powerful and influential China. As one put it in a particularly candid moment, "We want China to become the benevolent leader of the whole world."

China's growing nationalism is manifested in several specific issues. Strategically, it can be seen in Beijing's desire to be an independent and influential force in international affairs. China has foresworn an alliance, or even a close strategic alignment, with either superpower. As Party General Secretary Hu Yaobang declared at the Twelfth Party Congress in 1982, China will never "attach itself to any

[2]Deng Xiaoping, "Speech at the Third Plenary Session of the Central Advisory Commission of the Communist Party of China," in Deng, *Build Socialism with Chinese Characteristics* (Beijing: Foreign Languages Press, 1985), p. 60.

big power or group of powers."[3] From this independent position, Beijing hopes to exercise greater influence over developments in East Asia. China is playing a more active role in discussions of regional economic and political issues, and its policy toward Vietnam reflects China's refusal to accept any outcome on its periphery that it considers detrimental to its interests. Moreover, although Beijing presently assigns a relatively low priority to military modernization, it is clear that Chinese leaders intend gradually to build a more powerful and effective military force.

In the economic and cultural spheres, Chinese nationalism is apparent in Beijing's attempt to avoid dependence on any foreign trading partner, its desire to protect domestic industry from foreign competition, and its insistence that China receive equal, if not preferential, treatment in international markets. The goal of preserving a national cultural essence—of building "socialism with Chinese characteristics"—even as China adopts some values and institutions from abroad, can also be seen as a form of cultural nationalism. So too are the recent criticisms of "bourgeois liberalization," "national nihilism," and "all-around Westernization."

One of the classic manifestations of modern nationalism involves territorial issues. Beijing shows no signs of seeking any major changes in the national boundaries of China established in the late nineteenth and early twentieth centuries, even though it regards many of the treaties that determined those borders to have been unequal and unjust. Thus, China lays no current claim to large parts of Siberia or to Outer Mongolia, even though these territories were wrested from Chinese control by Russia between 1860 and 1920. But Beijing still has differences with many of its neighbors on smaller territorial issues: with the Soviet Union over the islands in the Amur and Ussuri Rivers and over the Pamir Mountains, with India over parts of Kashmir and the Northeast Frontier Agency, with Japan over the Senkaku (or Diaoyutai) islands off the coast of Taiwan, and with Vietnam over the land boundary between the two countries and over the islands in the South China Sea.

Moreover, Deng Xiaoping has assigned high priority to the goal of national reunification, which he has described as one of the country's principal tasks for the 1980s and 1990s. The agreements that China signed with Britain concerning Hong Kong and with Portugal regarding Macao provide that these two territories will be returned to

[3]Hu Yaobang, "Create a New Situation in All Fields of Socialist Modernization," in *The Twelfth National Congress of the CPC (September 1982)* (Beijing: Foreign Languages Press, 1982), p. 55.

Chinese sovereignty by the turn of the century. Clearly, Deng would like to see comparable progress on the Taiwan question as well. Although it is unlikely that the unification of Taiwan and the mainland can occur by the year 2000, Beijing is pressing for the initiation of negotiations on the subject, or at least for the opening of unofficial commercial and cultural ties across the Taiwan Strait.

In several ways, therefore, the current period in China's foreign relations is without precedent. For the first time in its history, China is governed by an effective, consolidated government that has identified economic modernization as its highest priority. For the first time since the late eighteenth century, China has regained a prestigious and powerful position in international affairs and is relatively secure from direct foreign invasion. And for the first time since 1949, China has accepted the legitimacy of the international order and is seeking normal and stable relations with both of the superpowers.

To be sure, there are important continuities with the past. Chinese leaders continue to see international politics as a struggle against the hegemonism of major powers and to depict China as a supporter of the Third World in its quest for security, peace, and development. China is still sensitive to the preservation of its national sovereignty in an increasingly interdependent world and still seeks to complete the task of regaining control over territories lost to foreign powers and rival domestic governments. Beijing continues to adopt the role of a *demandeur* in international affairs, expressing moral indignation at any signs that it is being treated unequally or unfairly by other powers. But despite these links to earlier periods in its foreign relations, the present era in Chinese foreign policy is unprecedented for its emphasis on maintaining a network of international relationships that will support a sustained drive toward economic modernization.

The new era in Chinese foreign policy, then, blends peaceful coexistence, economic cooperation, and diplomatic flexibility together with territorial, economic, and strategic nationalism. It is this combination of divergent tendencies that helps explain the ambivalent attitudes toward China that prevail in so much of Asia. China's neighbors welcome the fact that Beijing's dedication to the tasks of economic development and reform is producing an interest in a peaceful international environment, global prosperity, and conciliatory relations with virtually every other country in the region. But over the longer term, China's modernization means that Beijing will have greater material resources with which to pursue its international objectives, and growing Chinese nationalism raises the possibility that those goals may be defined in ways that compete or conflict with the interests of other Asian states.

16

III. China Looks at Northeast Asia

Virtually all these generalizations about the new era in Chinese foreign policy are manifested in China's relations with Northeast Asia. China's acceptance of the legitimacy of the international order is reflected in its recent involvement in such institutions as the Asian Development Bank, the Pacific Economic Cooperation Conference, and the Asian Games. The growing importance of economics in China's foreign relations is demonstrated by the expansion of its trade not only with Japan and Hong Kong, but also with Taiwan and South Korea. The PRC's desire for a peaceful international environment is nowhere better exemplified than by the recent reduction in tensions in its relations with the Soviet Union and by its continuing efforts to prevent a renewal of conflict on the Korean peninsula. And Beijing's growing pragmatism can be seen in its more realistic attitude toward Taiwan and in its flexibility in its negotiations with Great Britain over the future of Hong Kong.

At the same time, however, China's relations with Northeast Asia also reflect the nationalistic character of contemporary Chinese foreign policy. China's desire to avoid strategic dependence on the United States and to strike a independent posture in international affairs is one reason for its recent rapprochement with the Soviet Union. The apprehension of many Chinese about excessive economic reliance upon foreign countries has contributed to recent tensions in China's relations with Japan, including protests by university students against what they charged was a "second Japanese invasion" of their country. The long-standing concern with the contamination of Chinese culture by influences from the outside is focused, to a large degree, on the extensive relations now developing with Hong Kong, with some senior Chinese officials warning against what they describe as the "Hong Kongization" of Southeast China. The growing desire to reunify China after more than a century of disunity is reflected in the concentration of Chinese leaders on solving the issues of Hong Kong and Macao by the end of the century. And Chinese concern that both the United States and Japan would prefer to preserve an independent Taiwan has been a recurrent irritant in its relations with Washington and, more recently, with Tokyo as well.

Before assessing China's bilateral relations with the major countries and territories of Northeast Asia, we should first examine Beijing's perception of the region as a whole. Interestingly, Chinese view the region in ways that are not too far different from the prevailing

17

assessments in the United States or Japan. Most Chinese are concerned with the rise of Soviet military presence in the region, although they are also increasingly troubled by some of the countermeasures being taken by Japan and, to a lesser degree, the United States. They are also impressed with the dynamism of most of the economies of Northeast Asia, although they warn of growing tensions in the economic relations between the developing nations of the Western Pacific and the United States and Japan.

Like many Americans, the Chinese usually begin their analysis of Northeast Asia with attention to the extraordinary pace of economic development in most parts of the region—particularly Japan, South Korea, Taiwan, Hong Kong, and now China itself—over the last ten to twenty years. When juxtaposed to the less dramatic rates of growth elsewhere, particularly in Europe and Latin America, the dynamism of Northeast Asia is giving that region an increasing role in the global economy and a growing place in world politics. The Chinese differ among themselves in their views of the relative importance of Europe and Asia, but there appears to be consensus on a critical point: even if Europe remains the focus of the strategic confrontation between the two superpowers and even if the Atlantic remains the center of the world economy, Asia is rapidly rising to a nearly equal status.

In recognition of the region's increasing strategic significance, Chinese analysts believe, the two superpowers are devoting considerable attention to bolstering their military and political position in Northeast Asia. As they have for the past ten years, the Chinese portray the Soviet Union as engaged in a strategic offensive in Asia, strengthening its military forces in Siberia, building a more extensive military relationship with Vietnam and North Korea, and seeking to weaken or disrupt American alliances. The Chinese see the United States on the defensive in Asia but rising more effectively than before to meet the Soviet challenge. Recent Chinese analyses have noted the expansion and modernization of American naval and air forces in the Western Pacific, the growing military cooperation between the United States and Japan, and the solidification of strategic ties between Washington and Seoul.

On balance, the Chinese view the strategic situation in Northeast Asia as relatively stable. From their perspective, the Korean peninsula is the one place in the region where a war might break out, but Beijing professes confidence that the North Koreans will not launch a major attack against their rivals to the south. Still, the Chinese express concern about what they regard as a growing arms race by the superpowers in Northeast Asia. The growing Soviet deployments in Siberia, including a substantial portion of the Soviet Union's ballistic-missile submarine force, makes it an attractive target for an American strike. At the same time, Beijing is well aware of the American concept of "horizontal escalation," in which the United States would retaliate, in Northeast Asia, against a limited war launched by the Soviet Union in some other part of the world. Thus, while a world war is not likely to begin in Northeast Asia, it could rapidly extend there from another region. And it is this prospect that causes disquiet in Beijing.

When viewing the general economic trends in Northeast Asia, Chinese analysts acknowledge that the success of most Northeast Asian economies has meant that North-South issues have thus far been relatively muted in this part of the world. But Beijing foresees increasing tension in the economic relations within the region as the growth of world trade slackens from the rapid pace of the 1970s. In particular, Chinese specialists on international economic issues point to the growing dissatisfaction in the less developed economies of the region with the rising tide of protectionism in the United States and the remaining barriers in Japan against the import of manufactured goods. They perceive resentment in these countries against the penetration of the smaller economies by Japanese and American multinational corporations and against their dependence on Japanese and American suppliers for parts and equipment. Significantly, however, they do not regard China's own entry into the international marketplace as posing a threat to the smaller economies of the region. China, they say, will not compete with other Asian nations for foreign capital or markets. Instead, China's new openness to the international economy should provide greater opportunities for cooperation with the newly industrializing economies of the region.

Although the Chinese forecast growing economic conflicts in the Asia-Pacific region, they are cautious about the prospects for the creation of a single international institution that can ameliorate them. Like many other observers, the Chinese are convinced that the economic, social, and political differences among the nations of the region make it difficult, if not impossible, to agree on the composition of a single "Pacific Community." Like many developing economies, Beijing also worries that such an organization, if it were created, would become the forum in which Japan and the United States would seek to impose their solutions to regional economic issues. But, while skeptical about the feasibility of creating a single pan-Pacific organization, the Chinese are increasingly involved in a variety of regional discussion forums, ranging from bilateral dialogues with Japan, the United States, and Southeast Asia to multilateral conferences in which representatives from Taiwan and South Korea are also involved.

In short, the Chinese currently view Northeast Asia with considerable satisfaction. They see a relatively healthy economic environment, a rough stalemate between the two superpowers, and little prospect of military conflict beginning anywhere in the region. Moreover, China's relations with its neighbors in the region have improved notably over the past decade, largely as the result of China's own efforts to reduce tensions with the Soviet Union, to expand its relations with Japan, and to open a dialogue with South Korea. Still, looking farther to the future, the Chinese see troubles on the horizon, particularly the arms race between the United States and the Soviet Union, North-South tensions over economic matters, and the growing economic and military power of Japan. Weighing these diverse factors, one leading Chinese analyst of Asian affairs has sketched out two broad possibilities for the future of the region:

> If the trend toward détente and dialogue continues to develop, and if the nations of the Asian-Pacific region maintain their independence and sovereignty, do not suffer interference from outside, and encourage the United States and the Soviet Union to conduct negotiations, halt [their] military confrontation, and cut down on nuclear weapons, then the future for the Asian-Pacific region will be one of peace and stability. This is [one] possibility. . . . [But] if the trend toward tension and conflict continues to develop, if the U.S.–Soviet conflict intensifies, and if the nations of the Asian-Pacific region become involved in [that] superpower conflict, then the future for the Asian-Pacific region will be one of tension and chaos. This is also a possibility.[4]

China, the Soviet Union, and Mongolia

In the late 1970s, anti-Sovietism appeared to be the cornerstone of Chinese foreign policy. Beijing described the Soviet Union as a "social-imperialist" state that was seeking global hegemony. It called for a united front of all small and medium-sized nations against Moscow and even implied that the United States was eligible for membership in this anti-Soviet alignment. It accused the Kremlin of trying to encircle and isolate China through its "southward thrusts" into Vietnam and, at the end of 1979, into Afghanistan. And it described the Soviet Union, rather than the United States, as the

---

[4]Pei Monong, "The Situation and Existing Problems in the Asian-Pacific Region," *Guoji Wenti Yanjiu*, no. 4 (October 1985), pp. 12-14, in *Foreign Broadcast Information Service Daily Report: China* (hereafter cited as *FBIS*), December 13, 1985, pp. A2-5, at p. A5.

principal threat to Chinese security. The tension between the two countries was symbolized by two events in 1979: the Chinese invasion of Vietnam, Moscow's ally, to "punish" Hanoi for its intervention in Cambodia; and Beijing's announcement that it would allow its own treaty of alliance with the Soviet Union to expire after its 30-year term ended in 1980.

In the early 1980s, however, China began to adopt a considerably more flexible and conciliatory posture toward the Soviet Union. In part, this was a response to a speech given by Leonid Brezhnev in Tashkent in early 1982, in which the Soviet leader provided a comprehensive statement of the Kremlin's policy toward China. Brezhnev said that the Soviet Union acknowledged China to be a socialist country and denied that Moscow posed any threat to China's security. He pointed out that, unlike the United States, the Soviet Union had consistently supported Beijing's position on the Taiwan question, accepting the PRC's claim that Taiwan was part of China. He also offered to discuss a resolution of the border dispute between the two countries and to resume economic, scientific, cultural, and political relations across the Sino-Soviet frontier.

The initial Chinese response was guarded. At the Twelfth Congress of the Chinese Communist Party the following August, General Secretary Hu Yaobang acknowledged that Soviet leaders had "expressed more than once the desire to improve relations with China" but said that Beijing considered "deeds, rather than words" to be the true measure of Soviet intentions. He listed three Soviet policies that China regarded as obstacles to the improvement of Sino-Soviet relations: the stationing of "massive armed forces" along the Sino-Soviet and Sino-Mongolian frontiers in the 1960s and 1970s; Moscow's support for Vietnam's "invasion and occupation" of Cambodia; and the Soviet Union's own intervention in Afghanistan. Hu implied that only if these three obstacles were removed could there be any normalization of Sino-Soviet relations.[5]

Nevertheless, Hu Yaobang's speech announced a change in Chinese foreign policy that was reassuring to Moscow. Hu declared that China would adopt an "independent foreign policy" and would never "attach itself to any big power or group of powers." This implied that China was backing away from its previous notion of a united front with the United States against the Soviet Union. Moreover, Hu also pledged to apply the principle of peaceful coexistence to China's relations with socialist countries, presumably including the Soviet Union. In October the two countries resumed the negotiations

[5]Hu, "Create a New Situation," pp. 58-59.

over bilateral relations that had been suspended after the Soviet invasion of Afghanistan. What is more, the portrayal of the Soviet Union in the Chinese press began to become noticeably more evenhanded. While Chinese journals continued to criticize particular aspects of Soviet foreign policy, they no longer described the Soviet Union as a "social-imperialist" country.

Gradually, too, Beijing softened its terms for a normalization of relations with the Soviet Union. By 1984 it was clear that China was willing to revitalize its economic and cultural ties with Moscow, even in the absence of any progress in removing the three obstacles to Sino-Soviet relations. Trade between the two countries rose by 60 percent in 1984 to some $1.2 billion and then rose by another 75 percent the following year. Beijing accepted a Soviet offer to recommence technological assistance to China in the form of the modernization of some of the factories that Moscow had supplied to the PRC at the height of their economic cooperation in the mid-1950s. A joint commission on economic and scientific cooperation, chaired at the vice–prime ministerial level, was established to coordinate the expanded relationship. Exchanges of journalists, tourists, scholars, and parliamentary delegations resumed once again, although on a relatively modest scale. As one Communist newspaper in Hong Kong described the situation, "the political differences [between China and the Soviet Union] will not affect the development of economic and other relations between them."[6]

Although the Chinese continued to insist that there be some progress on removing the three obstacles before there could be a full normalization of political relations between the two countries—defined as a summit meeting between Chinese and Soviet leaders, routine discussions between their foreign ministers, or the resumption of party-to-party relations—even here there was a subtle easing of the Chinese position. In 1982 Hu Yaobang had implied that all three obstacles would have to be removed before there could be any improvement in Sino-Soviet relations, but by mid-1985 Chinese spokesmen were saying that Moscow needed to make concessions on only one of the three obstacles for there to be progress toward political normalization. There appeared to be some differences of opinion as to which of the three obstacles should be tackled first. Some leaders implied it should be the buildup of Soviet forces along the border with China; others, including Deng Xiaoping, said it should be Soviet support for Vietnamese policy in Cambodia. Nonetheless, the reduction of the Chinese terms for political normalization

[6]*Ta Kung Pac*, July 12, 1985, p. 2, in *FBIS*, July 12, 1985, pp. W1-2.

from the removal of all three obstacles to the addressing of but one represented a further gesture toward the Soviet Union.

It remains to explain why China would take a more relaxed posture toward Moscow in the 1980s than in the 1970s. One reason is that China feels more secure now than it did then. Beijing believes that the Soviet Union has largely spent the international momentum it generated in the 1970s, is increasingly preoccupied with its domestic economic problems, and has been counterbalanced by the growth of American military power during the Reagan administration. Further, the Chinese have also concluded that the greater internal stability and economic growth that have been achieved in the post-Mao era make the PRC a much less attractive target for Soviet pressure.

In addition, the Chinese see compelling economic grounds for a reduction of tensions with the Soviet Union. As indicated in the previous section, Beijing wants a peaceful international environment so that it can devote all available resources to the task of economic development and reform. And, more specifically, China can benefit in a variety of ways from access to the economies of the Soviet Union and Eastern Europe. Technology from the Soviet bloc can be used to update equipment that was imported from the USSR and Eastern Europe in the 1950s. The economic reforms undertaken in such countries as Hungary, East Germany, and even the Soviet Union itself since the mid-1960s provide useful lessons—although not necessarily adaptable models—for Beijing's own experiments in economic restructuring. Moreover, the prospect of an "open door" to the Soviet Union is of appeal to those interior provinces in China, particularly in the northwest, which have little hope of benefiting as much as the coastal regions from the opening to Japan and the United States.

Finally, there is a persuasive political calculus to the reorientation of Chinese foreign policy. The previous posture of a "united front" with the United States against the Soviet Union was controversial on several grounds: It threatened to embroil China in a potential Soviet-American dispute; it reduced Beijing's leverage over the United States on the Taiwan issue; and it was an unnecessary irritant to the PRC's relations with the Soviet Union. Perhaps most fundamentally, a policy of alignment with the United States—a country which many Chinese still regard as, in some sense, an imperialist power—attracts much less domestic support in China than does a policy of strategic independence. China's policy of the 1970s offered alignment with one superpower and confrontation with the other. In contrast, its contemporary international posture promises to avoid the entanglements of either alliance or conflict, while engaging in dialogue with both.

While welcoming China's willingness to improve its economic and cultural relations with the Soviet Union, Moscow initially refused to meet Beijing's terms for the normalization of political ties between the two countries. The Kremlin continued to press for a meeting of the foreign ministers of the two nations, proposed a summit conference, and suggested a series of confidence-building measures along the Sino-Soviet border. But the Soviet Union refused to make any concessions on any of the three obstacles on the grounds that they involved relations with third countries that were inappropriate to discuss with Beijing. The Soviet Union appeared to believe that, having dropped any preconditions for the restoration of economic relations, Beijing would ultimately reach a similar conclusion about the normalization of its political ties with Moscow.

But in July 1986 Mikhail Gorbachev announced a significant change in Soviet policy toward China. In a speech at Vladivostok—every bit as significant a milestone in the evolution of Soviet policy toward China as Brezhnev's address at Tashkent four years earlier—Gorbachev promised concessions on two of China's three obstacles. He announced the imminent withdrawal of six Soviet regiments from Afghanistan, promised the removal of a significant portion of the Soviet troops in Mongolia, and indicated a willingness to negotiate with China a balanced and mutual reduction of the remaining forces along the Sino-Soviet frontier. Gorbachev also reemphasized some earlier Soviet proposals for the improvement of bilateral relations between Moscow and Beijing, including the negotiation of a new agreement that would accept China's interpretation of the location of the riverine boundaries between the two countries.

China's response to the Gorbachev speech was, in its basic tone, similar to that to the Brezhnev address in Tashkent: it was cool but showed some signs of interest. Once again, Chinese spokesmen pointed out that Gorbachev had made only verbal promises and that they were waiting to see whether his words would be transformed into action. They questioned the significance of the Soviet leader's initiatives, belittling the scale of the proposed Soviet withdrawal from Afghanistan and noting that any Soviet forces removed from Mongolia could easily be reintroduced on very short notice. Most important of all, they pointed out that Gorbachev had made no concessions on the third obstacle—Soviet support for the Vietnamese invasion of Cambodia—which they now explicitly identified as the issue of greatest concern to Beijing. Even so, commenting on the Gorbachev speech in an interview on American television some weeks later,

Deng Xiaoping acknowledged that the Soviet leader's remarks had "contained something new." Deng even promised to come out of partial retirement and travel to the Soviet Union to meet Gorbachev if the Soviet Union secured the removal of Vietnamese troops from Cambodia.

By the autumn of 1986, therefore, China and the Soviet Union were engaged in serious negotiations over the full normalization of their political relations. How far the process will unfold will depend on the extent to which each side is flexible and forthcoming. China will be waiting to see whether the Soviet Union will actually implement the withdrawal of Soviet forces from Afghanistan and Mongolia that was pledged in the Gorbachev speech in Vladivostok and, equally important, whether Moscow will begin to dissociate itself from Hanoi's invasion of Cambodia. For its part, the Soviet Union will be waiting to see whether Beijing will adopt an equidistant posture toward the two superpowers or whether it will maintain a noticeable tilt toward the United States. The interplay of these two sets of calculations will determine whether the Sino-Soviet détente of the last several years halts roughly where it is or whether it evolves into a closer Sino-Soviet relationship.

Although Beijing's policy toward Moscow will therefore be strongly influenced by the future decisions of the Kremlin, it is possible to sketch out some of its likely parameters. It is highly likely that, given even a modest amount of additional Soviet flexibility, China will agree to a formal foreign ministers' meeting, and even to a summit conference—although not necessarily a dramatic meeting between Deng and Gorbachev inside the Soviet Union. Further Soviet concessions might earn a restoration of party-to-party relations and, possibly, public acknowledgment by the Chinese that Beijing and Moscow hold common positions on certain regional and global issues.

But there will also be limits on how far Beijing will move toward a true rapprochement with the Soviet Union. Chinese leaders have already indicated, publicly and explicitly, that there can be no return to the kind of Sino-Soviet relationship that existed in the 1950s. China's forswearing of a comprehensive security relationship with any superpower refers as much to the Soviet Union as to the United States; and Beijing has made clear that the resumption of formal relations between the two Communist parties will not mean acknowledgment of Soviet leadership of the socialist camp.

In addition, the amelioration of Sino-Soviet relations will also be limited by China's ties to the United States. By welcoming Defense Secretary Caspar Weinberger to Beijing in October 1986, only two months after the Gorbachev speech in Vladivostok, the PRC put the

Soviet Union on notice that an improvement in Sino-Soviet ties would not necessarily lead to the termination of a low-key but steadily developing military relationship between the United States and China. Nor would Beijing want the reduction of tensions with the Soviet Union to cause any slackening of American cooperation with China's civilian modernization program.

Finally, there are no indications that China has altered its underlying perception that the Soviet Union remains the principal threat to its national security. And there are only two developments that might cause Beijing to change this assessment. One would be a fundamental deterioration of Sino-American relations, particularly with regard to the Taiwan question; the other would be the abandonment of the Soviet Union's efforts to expand its military power and political influence in East Asia. While each development is conceivable, neither is likely. Neither the United States nor the PRC is apt to scuttle their bilateral relations over the Taiwan issue. Nor is the Soviet Union likely to give up its competition with the United States in Asia for the sake of mollifying the Chinese.

Before turning to China's policy toward Japan, it is necessary briefly to address Beijing's relations with Mongolia. The Chinese disclaim any territorial ambitions with regard to Mongolia and insist that they fully accept the existence of an independent Mongolian state. What concerns Beijing is the presence of large numbers of Soviet forces in Mongolia, placed there beginning in 1967, which pose a threat to the security of all of north and northeast China. The close military relationship between the Soviet Union and Mongolia has led China to regard Ulan Bator as little more than a client state of Moscow. In the late 1960s and 1970s, therefore, the political and economic relationship between China and Mongolia deteriorated along with the relations between China and the Soviet Union.

The recent improvement in Sino-Soviet relations has been accompanied by some amelioration in Sino-Mongolian ties. Trade between the two countries has resumed, albeit at extremely low levels. Air service between Beijing and Ulan Bator, suspended at the nadir of Sino-Mongolian relations, has been reinstated, at least during the summer months. The two countries have reached an agreement on managing some of their border disputes; and a political dialogue between the two nations has resumed, with China dispatching a vice foreign minister and a high-level parliamentary delegation to Ulan Bator. The Chinese have presumably used these opportunities to reassure the Mongols that no untoward consequences will result from the withdrawal of Soviet forces. Still, although China apparently seeks a normal relationship with Mongolia, it is evident, as we will see in the next chapter, that Ulan Bator remains highly suspicious of long-term Chinese intentions.

China and Japan

One of the most tragic features of the international relations of East Asia was the rivalry between China and Japan from the end of the nineteenth century to the middle of the twentieth. Historically, most Chinese, and many Japanese, regarded Japan as a tributary state of China—culturally dependent, geographically peripheral, and politically submissive. But the relationship between the two countries changed fundamentally in the latter half of the nineteenth century, when Japan was able to embark on a sustained and effective program of modernization, while China remained ensnared in a series of abortive reforms and disruptive revolutions. The growing rivalry between a rising Japan and a declining China was reflected in a war over Korea and Taiwan in 1894-95, a series of Japanese demands for political and economic concessions in the 1910s and 1920s, the Japanese seizure of Manchuria in 1928, and then an all-out Japanese invasion of China in 1937.

Japan's defeat in 1945 and the Communist victory in China in 1949 transformed the relationship between the two countries from one of direct military confrontation to something considerably more complex. Politically, China and Japan remained adversaries. Under pressure from the United States and with the support of many conservatives in Japan, Tokyo refrained from establishing diplomatic relations with the Communist government in Beijing, signed a peace treaty with Taiwan, and continued to recognize the Nationalists in Taipei as the government of all China. Because of this, and because of Japan's military alliance with the United States, Beijing regarded Tokyo as a subordinate but critical component in the American scheme to isolate and contain the PRC. In turn, China's alliance with the Soviet Union was, at least in name, directed against the possible resurgence of aggression on the part of Japan.

Although the political relations between China and Japan remained seriously strained, economic ties between the two countries developed rapidly. Like China today, Japan in the 1950s and 1960s devoted itself to the task of economic recovery and modernization, and, to that end, was eager to separate politics and economics to the greatest degree possible. As a result, the absence of diplomatic relations between China and Japan did not deter Tokyo from attempting to expand its economic relations with the PRC. Although there were

27

periods in the late 1950s when China was reluctant to trade with the Japanese without significant political concessions from Tokyo, by the early 1960s Beijing had decided to accept the Japanese principle of separating trade from diplomacy. Accordingly, Chinese imports from Japan rose from $2.8 million in 1960 to $257 million in 1965—nearly a ten-fold increase—and Japan supplanted the Soviet Union as China's largest trading partner.

The development of Sino-Japanese economic contacts laid the foundation for the normalization of diplomatic relations between the two countries. Henry Kissinger's visit to Beijing in July 1971 gave the Japanese dramatic evidence that the United States would no longer resist political ties between Japan and China. Within a few months of the Kissinger visit, Tokyo and Beijing had established formal diplomatic relations. By 1978 the two countries had negotiated a treaty of peace and friendship, which officially brought to an end their military confrontation of the 1930s and 1940s.

The normalization of political relations between Japan and China was facilitated by the fact that the two countries had developed similar perspectives on a number of critical issues in the Asia-Pacific region. By 1978 both had become concerned about the expansion of Soviet military power in East Asia and about Soviet attempts to translate its burgeoning military force into expanded political influence. The Chinese supported Japan's claim to four northern islands occupied by the Soviet Union at the end of World War II, and Japan joined China in opposing the Vietnamese invasion of Cambodia at the end of 1978. By then Tokyo and Beijing had strong ties with the United States, and both supported a vigorous and effective American political and military presence in East Asia as a counterbalance to the Soviet Union.

Given the natural complementarity between the two economies, China's decision in the 1970s to greatly expand its foreign economic relations produced a further surge in Sino-Japanese trade. Two-way trade, which had amounted to $480 million in 1965, rose to $3.8 billion in 1975 and to $20 billion in 1985. This expansion was facilitated by agreements on technological cooperation in several key sectors of the Chinese economy, including steel, transportation, and energy, and by official Japanese loans and export credits totaling some $8 billion by 1985. By the middle of the 1980s China purchased about one-third of its imports from Japan and sold about a quarter of its exports on the Japanese market.

The convergence of the economic and strategic interests of Japan and China was reflected in the frequent exchanges of high-level visits between the two countries. Deng Xiaoping, Zhao Ziyang, and Hu

Yaobang all traveled to Japan at various times after 1978, and Prime Ministers Ohira, Suzuki, and Nakasone paid return visits to China. A ministerial-level commission was established to coordinate the economic and technological relationship between the two countries. Given these important developments, it is understandable that both Chinese and Japanese spokesmen describe the mid-1980s as the most stable and friendly period in Sino-Japanese relations in more than a hundred years.

Beneath the surface, however, Sino-Japanese relations remain somewhat fragile, largely because the mistrust created by 50 years of military confrontation and reinforced by nearly 25 more years of political isolation cannot readily be eased. Japanese concerns about China will be discussed in some detail in the next chapter. At this point, it is appropriate to summarize four of the most important problems that shape Chinese perceptions of Japan: the possible resurgence of Japanese militarism, the imbalanced economic relationship between the two countries, the lingering differences over Taiwan, and a territorial dispute between China and Japan over some islands just northeast of Taiwan. Of these four, the first two are issues of immediate importance while the latter two are potential problems that might assume greater significance in the years ahead.

Like much of the rest of East Asia—particularly those countries that experienced Japanese colonialization or invasion between 1895 and 1945—China remains apprehensive about the resurgence of Japanese military power as Tokyo assumes a more active role in regional and global affairs. To be sure, the improvements in Sino-American and Sino-Japanese relations over the last fifteen years, the continuing strength of the Japanese-American strategic relationship, and the gradual pace of Japanese military buildup have somewhat assuaged Chinese concerns. At least in the short run, Beijing can be reasonably confident that the Japanese policy is not directed against China and will be closely coordinated with that of the United States.

Even so, Chinese officials and analysts have frequently expressed the opinion that Japanese rearmament should be limited to what is needed for the country's self-defense. In August 1985, for example, Vice-Premier Yao Yilin said that Japanese defense preparations that went beyond the requirements of self-defense would "arouse and upset Japan's neighbors," presumably including China.[7] A year later, the Chinese Ministry of Foreign Affairs, in commenting on a Japanese long-range defense plan, noted that while "Japan has the right to self-defense," its military capabilities "should be moderate and

[7]Xinhua News Agency, August 27, 1985, in *FBIS*, August 27, 1985, p. D1.

should not cause concern to its neighboring countries."[8] When, in early 1987, the Japanese government announced that national defense spending would finally exceed one percent of Japan's GNP—a ceiling that had remained intact for more than a decade—the Chinese response was sharper still. The Ministry of Foreign Affairs officially expressed its "concern" over the development, while a Communist newspaper in Hong Kong declared that the spending increase revealed Japan's "expansionist ambitions" and urged the victims of past Japanese aggression to "heighten their vigilance."[9]

While they have devoted considerable attention to monitoring the Japanese military development program, Chinese observers have expressed even greater anxiety about what they see as the rise of nationalism in contemporary Japan. (This attitude stands in sharp contrast to the prevailing opinion in the United States, which regards Japan as a pacifist nation that has refused to bear its fair share of the burden of its own defense.) As evidence for its apprehensions, Beijing points to the visits of high-level Japanese officials, including Prime Minister Nakasone, to the Yasukuni Shrine in Tokyo, which commemorates some Japanese war criminals as well as ordinary officers and soldiers. The Chinese have also indicated their disapproval of the efforts by some conservative and nationalistic groups in Japan to publish textbooks which, in Beijing's opinion, exonerate Japanese colonialism and expansion in Asia in the first half of the century and downplay Japanese atrocities during World War II.

Responsible Chinese analysts are cautious in characterizing these recent trends in Japan. Although a number are willing to conclude that "great power chauvinism" is on the increase in Japan, relatively few are prepared to argue that there has been a resurgence of militarism in Japan or that such a development is likely to occur in the near future. Nonetheless, many Chinese are worried that the revival of Japanese nationalism had the support of Prime Minister Nakasone and that it will be accelerated by the rise of a younger generation of Japanese who lack direct experience of World War II and who have become emboldened by Japan's recent economic dominance. At least one Chinese analyst has described the emergence of Japanese nationalism as a "potential obstacle" to the smooth development of Sino-Japanese relations.

A second issue that has complicated Sino-Japanese relations in recent months has been the economic ties between the two countries.

[8]Agence France Presse, August 12, 1986, in *FBIS*, August 12, 1986, p. D1.

[9]Xinhua News Agency, January 2, 1987, in *FBIS*, January 2, 1987, p. D1; and *Wen Wei Po*, January 3, 1987, in *FBIS*, January 7, 1987, pp. D1-2.

The expansion in trade between China and Japan over the last decade has, not surprisingly, produced tensions between China and Japan that resemble those that Japan has experienced with its other trading partners in the Third World. The greatest irritant has been the large deficits in China's trade with Japan since 1983: $1.3 billion in 1984, $6.0 billion in 1985, and $4.2 billion in 1986. These have been largely due to a surge of Chinese imports, caused by large bonuses and wage increases at the end of 1984, an excessive level of domestic investment, and the loosening of central controls over foreign trade. But the Chinese, like many of Japan's other trading partners, also complain that the restrictions on access to the Japanese market make it impossible for China to increase its exports to Japan as rapidly as its imports.

Beijing has also raised some other grievances about its economic relations with Japan. The Chinese complain that Japanese entrepreneurs have lagged behind the United States in making direct investments in China and have been reluctant to transfer advanced technology to the PRC. The Chinese have also criticized several common Japanese trading practices, including providing lower-quality products to customers who had insisted on paying a lower price and charging high prices for spare parts and components required by Chinese enterprises that have imported Japanese equipment and assembly lines.

The emotions produced by these two issues—the rise of Japanese nationalism and the tensions in Sino-Japanese economic relations—were evident in the anti-Japanese demonstrations by university students that erupted in several Chinese cities in September and October 1985. The Chinese government depicted the protests as directed against the revival of Japanese militarism, and this was indeed one aspect of the student movement. But the students also criticized what some called the "second Japanese invasion of China": the flood of Japanese consumer goods in China's coastal cities and the prevalence of advertisements for Japanese products on Chinese billboards and on Chinese television. Given the fact that Beijing wished to encourage larger amounts of Japanese investment in China, Chinese leaders were less eager to publicize this second theme of the student protest.

Since 1985, Taiwan has assumed growing prominence as a third issue in Sino-Japanese relations, albeit one that is still less important than Japanese defense spending or China's trade deficit with Tokyo. Although the Japanese government transferred diplomatic recognition from Taipei to Beijing in 1972, the Kuomintang on Taiwan retains substantial support in Japan, particularly among the parliamentary delegation of the ruling Liberal Democratic Party. The executive branch of the Japanese government has refused to maintain any official relations with Taiwan. But other parts of the Japanese establishment have not been as strict. In 1985 a number of LDP politicians agreed to participate in a ceremony in Taipei commemorating the hundredth anniversary of the birth of Chiang Kai-shek. After Chinese complaints, the Gaimushō assured Beijing that these were private activities that did not represent official Japanese policy, and the incident passed without significant repercussions. In early 1987, however, a district court in Osaka ruled that a student dormitory in Kyoto still belonged to the Nationalist government on Taiwan, which had purchased it after World War II, rather than to the Communist government in Beijing. This occasioned a strong Chinese protest, with commentators in Beijing charging that Tokyo had implicitly adopted a "two-China policy." It may also have led Deng Xiaoping to warn that other countries—presumably implying Japan as well as the United States—might try to "take it [Taiwan] away" from China.[10]

A final irritant in Sino-Japanese relations involves conflicting claims to a group of small islands, known in Chinese as the Diaoyutai and in Japanese as the Senkakus. Located just northeast of Taiwan, these uninhabited islets, which are presently controlled by the Japanese, serve as a haven for fishermen and sit atop vast quantities of natural resources under the ocean floor. A minor incident occurred in 1978, during the negotiations over the Sino-Japanese treaty of peace and friendship, when a flotilla of armed Chinese fishing boats approached the islands displaying signs declaring that the "Diaoyutai are Chinese territory." After a quick round of negotiations, during which the Chinese government insisted that the incident was "accidental," the two sides agreed that the issue should be "shelved for the time being."[11] Nonetheless, it is not inconceivable that a more nationalistic China might choose to reassert its claim to the islands in the years ahead.

To manage these problems in Sino-Japanese relations, the two sides established a "21st Century Committee for China-Japan Friendship" during Prime Minister Nakasone's visit to China in 1984. This committee, composed of leading citizens from both countries, is supposed to hold regular meetings to review Sino-Japanese relations and to make recommendations to the two governments. As part of the committee's work, General Secretary Hu Yaobang invited a

---

[10]Xinhua News Agency, April 17, 1987, in FBIS, April 17, 1987, p. U1.

[11]Shinkichi Eto, "Recent Developments in Sino-Japanese Relations," *Asian Survey* XX:7 (July 1980), pp. 726-43.

delegation of 3,000 Japanese youths to visit China in late 1984. Ironically, this gesture itself became the focus of criticism inside China on the grounds that it was unseemly, expensive, and ultimately an ineffective attempt to curry favor among young Japanese. Indeed, the issue was a minor factor in the forced resignation of Hu Yaobang in January 1987.

On balance, there has been a substantial congruence in Chinese and Japanese interests, both strategic and economic, since the early 1970s. As a result, the conflicts that dominated the relations between the two countries for the previous hundred years have largely been superseded by a more cooperative relationship. Nonetheless, there remains in China a considerable degree of resentment over Tokyo's economic policies, apprehension about Japanese military capabilities, and even suspicion about Japan's attitude toward Taiwan. By early 1987 these issues had combined to create the highest level of tension between the two countries in a decade. The complete disintegration of the Sino-Japanese relationship remains highly unlikely. Nevertheless, given these factors, maintaining stability in relations between Beijing and Tokyo will require considerable effort by both sides, aimed not only at resolving the immediate issues in their relationship but also at overcoming the mutual suspicions created by their historic rivalry.

China and the Two Koreas

China's policy toward the Korean peninsula well illustrates the interplay of old and new elements in contemporary Chinese foreign relations. On the one hand, Beijing's interest in maintaining stability along the DMZ (Demilitarized Zone) reflects its desire for a peaceful international environment, and its growing economic and cultural ties with South Korea reflect its willingness to separate economics from politics in its relations with former adversaries. But on the other hand, despite the improvement in China's relations with the United States and South Korea, Beijing retains strong links with the Communist regime in Pyongyang and maintains its sole formal military alliance with the North Koreans. Furthermore, despite the recent reduction in tensions between China and the Soviet Union, Beijing is reluctant to allow its relations with Pyongyang to deteriorate to the point that the North Koreans would decide to tilt away from China and toward the Kremlin.

The alliance between Beijing and Pyongyang was forged, of course, during the Korean War of 1950-53. This was not a conflict China wanted. Beijing was, in mid-1950, preoccupied with other, more pressing issues, particularly its attempts to promote the recovery of the battered Chinese economy, to consolidate its control over the Chinese mainland, and to complete the "liberation" of Tibet and Taiwan. Nonetheless, when American troops crossed the 38th parallel late in the summer of 1950, with the goal of reunifying Korea under non-Communist rule, China felt compelled to intervene. That decision was costly, not only in terms of blood and treasure, but also because of the resulting rigidification of Sino-American relations and the formalization of the American military commitment to Taiwan.

Despite its alliance with Pyongyang, the PRC differs with North Korea on several key issues. First, Beijing appears to share with the Soviet Union a disdain for the nature of North Korean society under Kim Il-sung. The DPRK is, after all, one of the few remaining Stalinist regimes in the Communist world. Although the Chinese officially endorse Kim Il-sung's claim that it was the South, and not the North, that initiated the conflict in June 1950, many Chinese specialists on international affairs privately admit that the North started the Korean war, and a Chinese-language version of the *Encyclopedia Britannica* recently published in Beijing comes very close to providing the first public acknowledgment of the same fact. Moreover, the Chinese regard with distaste Kim Il-sung's efforts to transfer power to his son, Kim Jong-il, with Communist newspapers in Hong Kong disparaging the North Korean succession arrangements as an attempt to create the world's first "socialist monarchy."

It is for this reason that the Chinese have done their best to encourage the North Koreans to follow a course of reform similar to that pursued by the PRC since 1978. The Chinese have taken every opportunity to describe China's program of economic reform to North Korean visitors and have encouraged officials from Pyongyang to visit China's special economic zones (SEZs). In recent months, Chinese analysts have claimed to see some evidence that North Korea is joining much of the rest of the socialist bloc in a program of economic liberalization. They point to North Korea's joint-venture law as a sign that Pyongyang is beginning to open its economy to the outside world and claim that the DPRK is beginning experiments with a household responsibility system in agriculture and with a restructuring of its system of industrial organization. They also assert that Pyongyang has begun discussions with Beijing concerning the creation of a special economic zone along the Sino-Korean border. It is not certain that these signs of internal liberalization and of an opening to the outside world are as significant as the Chinese portray them, but it is clear that such developments would mark a change in North

34

Korean policy in the directions that the Chinese have been vigorously advocating.

In a second difference in perspective, Beijing appears to have a stronger interest than Pyongyang in maintaining peace and stability on the Korean peninsula. Pyongyang has, since the early 1980s, followed a two-track policy in pursuing its ultimate objective of securing a unified Korea under Communist leadership. On the one hand, it has occasionally shown a willingness to engage in dialogue with the South Korean government over such issues as the reunion of divided families, the development of economic relations, and the exchange of parliamentary delegations. Since 1983, it has also proposed trilateral negotiations, in a variety of formats, with both Seoul and Washington over the withdrawal of American forces from Korea, the replacement of the 1953 armistice with a formal peace treaty, and the reduction of tensions along the DMZ. At the same time, however, North Korea has steadily developed the ability to use armed force and violence against South Korea in pursuit of the same goals. Pyongyang's attempt in October 1983 to assassinate President Chun Doo-hwan during a state visit to Rangoon, along with much of the South Korean cabinet, is the most blatant example of this facet of North Korean policy. The deployment of large numbers of North Korean forces in offensive formations very close to the DMZ, the ongoing efforts to dig tunnels under it, and the continuing infiltration of North Korean agents into the South are also evidence of this second element of Pyongyang's strategy.

China, in contrast, recognizes unqualifiedly that the resumption of hostilities on the Korean peninsula would seriously threaten its interest in maintaining a peaceful international environment and in devoting all its resources to the pursuit of economic modernization and reform. A North Korean attack against the South, whether by conventional or unconventional measures, would place Beijing in a critical dilemma. To support Pyongyang would, at the minimum, produce serious strains in China's relations with Washington and Tokyo and, in the worst case, could even lead to direct military confrontation with the United States. But to repudiate its alliance with North Korea would run the risk of driving Pyongyang into an even closer relationship with the Soviet Union.

Given these considerations, Chinese officials and analysts have repeatedly emphasized their hope that North Korea will rely on peaceful means in pursuing its goal of national unification. China has strongly endorsed Pyongyang's proposals for trilateral negotiations with the United States and South Korea, and it served as an intermediary through which the North Korean initiative was relayed to the United States in 1983-84. China also gave its enthusiastic support to the dialogue between North and South Korea on economic, cultural, and humanitarian issues that occurred in 1984-85.

China has used several additional mechanisms to encourage Kim Il-sung to eschew the use of force on the Korean peninsula. By publicizing North Korean statements favoring peaceful reunification of the country, the Chinese imply that they consider Pyongyang to have made binding commitments in this regard. Chinese spokesmen also warn that, in their estimate, North Korea would not be able to launch a successful attack against the South, given the strength of the ROK armed forces and the immediate involvement of the United States. As one Chinese analyst has put it, "no North Korean leader with any common sense" would attempt to use force against the South.

Furthermore, the Chinese have given clear indications to Pyongyang that Beijing would oppose any North Korean use of force against the South. While Beijing has refused to issue a formal condemnation of the North Korean assassination plot in Rangoon and has not yet officially acknowledged Pyongyang's responsibility, there are indications that the Chinese made strong representations to the DPRK criticizing this aspect of North Korean policy. In 1986, Deng Xiaoping told a visiting European leader that, given that the "overwhelming majority of the people of the world" want peace, any country launching a war "will not win support, even from his allies." Since China's sole alliance is with North Korea, Deng's statement strongly implied that the PRC would not back Pyongyang if the DPRK were again to initiate hostilities on the Korean peninsula.[12] Chinese sources also say that Deng made the same point more explicitly in the middle of 1987, when he said that Beijing would support North Korea against an attack by the South, but would oppose any southward thrust by North Korean forces.

A third difference between China and North Korea involves the burgeoning ties between Beijing and Seoul. Despite Pyongyang's objections, China has shown a determination to establish and maintain unofficial contacts with South Korea. From the economic perspective, an opening to Seoul provides a market for Chinese exports, a source of technology and consumer goods, and a channel for information about one of the most successful of the East Asian NICs. Politically, China also sees an advantage in establishing contacts with one of the principal parties to the Korean dispute and in gaining

[12]Xinhua News Agency, October 28, 1986, in *FBIS*, October 28, 1986, p. G4.

influence with one of the countries that may play an increasingly active role in regional affairs in the decades ahead.

The most visible and dramatic breakthrough in Chinese relations with South Korea was Beijing's willingness to negotiate directly with Seoul for the release of a Chinese airliner that was hijacked to the ROK in 1983. Since then, there have been a variety of other developments: a continuing dialogue between Chinese and South Korean scholars in third countries, Chinese attendance at conferences in third countries where South Koreans are present, South Korean participation in international meetings and sporting events held in the PRC, and, perhaps of the greatest symbolic importance, Chinese participation in the 1986 Asian Games and the 1988 Olympic Games in Seoul. Chinese trade with South Korea, at about $1 billion annually, now exceeds its trade with North Korea, which was estimated at about $514 million for 1986.[13] There is also evidence to suggest that some South Korean entrepreneurs have used Hong Kong as a base for making disguised investments in southern China and that middle-level Chinese officials occasionally travel to Seoul to meet with their South Korean counterparts.

Despite these differences in perspective, China has sought to avoid any deterioration in its relations with Pyongyang. Strong ties to the DPRK are essential if China is to be able to dissuade North Korea from attacking the South or from forging a close alignment with the Soviet Union. As a result, even as it has tried to restrain Pyongyang from using force against Seoul, persuade the DPRK to adopt a course of domestic reform, and forge extensive unofficial ties with South Korea, China has simultaneously attempted to pressure friendly relations with North Korea. It has done so, first, by maintaining a constant stream of high-level visitors to and from North Korea, in an effort to assure Pyongyang of the importance that China assigns to its relations with the DPRK. China continues to supply North Korea with relatively sophisticated military equipment including, in 1983, approximately twenty A-5 fighters, the Chinese equivalent of the MiG-21. Beijing has also invited Kim Jong-il to visit the PRC, thus suggesting that, whatever its reservations about the North Korean succession arrangements, it is prepared to acknowledge the younger Kim as the leader of the DPRK after the death of his father.

China's continuing ties to Pyongyang are also apparent in its support of a variety of North Korean policy initiatives and its rejection of proposals by Japan and the United States that are unacceptable to

[13]Takashi Uehara, "North Korea's External Trade in 1986," *JETRO China Newsletter*, no. 70 (September-October 1987), pp. 16-21.

the DPRK. China has rather consistently echoed North Korea in calling for the withdrawal of American troops from South Korea, in proposing a nuclear-free zone on the Korean peninsula, and in endorsing Kim Il-sung's concept of a Korea unified under some form of confederal government. Conversely, China has rejected American proposals for cross-recognition of the two Koreas by the major Northeast Asian powers, has opposed the simultaneous admission of Seoul and Pyongyang to the United Nations, and has refused to join with the United States in a quadrilateral negotiation with the two Korean governments.

To a degree, China has also permitted its policy toward South Korea to be limited by its concern about Pyongyang's sensibilities. From time to time, Beijing has cut back its economic relations with Seoul when confronted with strong objections from North Korea. The PRC has also made clear that it is not prepared to establish official trade offices with South Korea or officially to acknowledge any trade between the two countries. It is unlikely, too, that Beijing would accept an offer of diplomatic recognition from Seoul. In all these ways, Beijing has indicated that it will not allow its ties with South Korea to take on any formal or official overtones, even though it has developed its informal and unofficial relations with Seoul with enthusiasm and alacrity.

Although this aspect of Chinese policy is due, above all, to Beijing's desire to maintain friendly ties with Pyongyang, China is also sensitive to the possible analogy between the Korean situation and the question of Taiwan. Thus, any American initiatives that suggest the permanent division of the Korean peninsula into two separate states—such as those calling for cross-recognition of the two Koreas or for their simultaneous entry into the United Nations—are nearly as troubling to Beijing as they are to Pyongyang. In Pyongyang's eyes, the institutionalization of the status quo on the Korean peninsula significantly reduces the possibility of an eventual reunification of Korea under Communist leadership. And, from Beijing's perspective, such a step might also create the precedent for a similar solution to the Taiwan issue.

While Beijing has been faithful to many of Pyongyang's policy preferences, it is important to recognize that the PRC has not chosen, thus far at least, to make them major issues in China's relations with either the United States or Japan. Although Chinese spokesmen may tell Americans that they favor the withdrawal of U.S. troops from South Korea, they often qualify this by acknowledging that the process should be gradual or by pointing out that the American forces need only be removed as far as Japan. In the same way, while endorsing the DPRK's call for tripartite negotiations with the United States and South Korea, China has in no way suggested that American acceptance of this proposal is a prerequisite for continued progress in Sino-American relations.

This dual policy—supporting some North Korean policies while criticizing others and attempting to preserve friendly relations with Pyongyang while developing unofficial ties to Seoul—has not in recent years brought all the results that Beijing might have liked. It is true that, on the surface, PRC-DPRK ties remain cordial, with the frequent exchanges of high-level visitors producing renewed expressions of solidarity and friendship by the two governments. But there are also indications that North Korea has become highly suspicious of Chinese domestic policy, which it may well regard as revisionist, and particularly of its international orientation, which includes the desire for closer ties with the United States, Japan, and South Korea—the three countries which Pyongyang views as its principal enemies.

Furthermore, North Korea has chosen to engage in a significant improvement of its relations with Moscow, to the point that Pyongyang has allowed the Soviet navy to call at North Korean ports and has permitted the Soviet air force to fly through North Korean airspace on reconnaissance missions along the Chinese coast. In turn, the Soviet Union has given greater publicity and support to North Korea's diplomatic initiatives and has supplied advanced MiG-23 fighters to Pyongyang's arsenal. These developments reflect Moscow's assessment that the strains in DPRK-PRC relations offer an opportunity for the Soviet Union to increase its influence in this corner of Northeast Asia.

Chinese officials and scholars profess to view these developments with equanimity. They express confidence that the North Koreans will never seek an exclusive relationship with the Soviet Union and assert that the Soviet Union, like China, will act as a restraint against a North Korean assault on the South. They insist that the recent deliveries of Soviet arms to the DPRK will not alter the balance of power on the Korean peninsula. Moreover, they correctly point out that, as Sino-Soviet relations themselves improve, Beijing has less reason to be alarmed about an amelioration of the ties between Moscow and Pyongyang.

Nonetheless, some Chinese observers privately acknowledge their concern about the recent improvements in Soviet–North Korean ties. If they were to develop into a close strategic relationship, then China would face a situation in which all the Asian Communist countries (Mongolia, Vietnam, Laos, and North Korea), as well as the largest neighboring non-Communist state (India), were aligned with the

Soviet Union. Accordingly, some Communist newspapers in Hong Kong, echoing the comments of some Chinese analysts in Beijing, have occasionally described the growing warmth in Soviet relations with the DPRK as the "fourth obstacle" to an improvement in Sino-Soviet relations.

Simultaneously, the PRC has begun to make more urgent appeals to Washington to help extricate China from its predicament. Loath to abandon its unofficial ties with South Korea but apprehensive about the development of Soviet–North Korean relations, Beijing's approach has been to encourage the United States to adopt a more flexible policy toward Pyongyang. If Washington would agree to do so, then, in Beijing's calculations, China could gain greater credibility in the eyes of North Korea and could secure greater toleration of its own flirtation with Seoul. In recent months, therefore, Chinese spokesmen have urged the United States to accept Pyongyang's proposals for tripartite negotiations, ease its trade embargo against North Korea, expand its unofficial contacts with the DPRK, or reduce the scale of its annual military exercises in the South. Such a sign of good will, the Chinese insist, would meet with a prompt response from the DPRK, reinforce the tendencies toward liberalization and reform in Pyongyang, and dissuade North Korea from tilting too far toward the Soviet Union.

Washington's recent decision to allow its diplomats to engage in substantive discussions with their North Korean counterparts at diplomatic receptions or in other "neutral" settings was therefore received with enthusiasm in Beijing. So too were the hints that the United States would be willing to undertake other initiatives toward the DPRK, including a relaxation of its trade embargo, if Pyongyang resumed its dialogue with the South and agreed to participate in the Seoul Olympics. The fact that the United States chose to convey these messages through Beijing, during Secretary of State Shultz's visit to China in early March 1987, also helped to bolster China's standing with North Korea.

China and Its Irredenta

A final element in China's relations with Northeast Asia involves the three territories—Macao, Hong Kong, and Taiwan—which Beijing does not presently administer, but which it regards as part of China. Macao, ceded to Portugal by the Ming Dynasty in 1568, was the earliest European trading outpost on the Chinese coast. Hong Kong, a British colony, is an amalgam of three pieces of land: Hong Kong island, granted to London in 1842; the Kowloon peninsula, ceded to Britain in 1860; and the New Territories, leased to the United Kingdom in 1898 for a period of 99 years. Taiwan, which was seized by Japan as a result of the Sino-Japanese War of 1895, was returned to China in 1945. For almost 40 years, however, it has been the seat of the Nationalist government, which established its capital in Taipei after having been driven off the Chinese mainland in 1949. Regaining sovereignty over these three places has been identified by Chinese leaders as one of their principal objectives for the remainder of the century.

Throughout most of the 1950s, 1960s, and 1970s, the PRC devoted most of its energies to reunification with Taiwan, with Hong Kong and Macao receiving only sporadic attention. Depending largely on the domestic political climate on the mainland itself, Beijing alternated between two approaches to the Taiwan question. During some periods, the PRC opted for a diplomatic strategy, offering Nationalist officials high positions in the Beijing government in return for the reunification of Taiwan with the mainland. At other times, Beijing used military pressure, particularly against the Nationalist-held islands just off the Chinese coast, to demoralize Taiwan or to drive a wedge between Taipei and Washington.

At first, neither strategy worked. The Nationalists under Chiang Kai-shek refused to negotiate with the Communists, and the use of military pressure by the PRC failed to weaken either Taipei's resolve or the political connection between Taiwan and the United States. Then, in the late 1970s, China scored a significant victory. In 1978 the United States agreed to switch its diplomatic relations from the Nationalist government in Taipei to the Communist government in Beijing. As part of this decision, Washington also announced the termination of its Mutual Defense Treaty with Taiwan and the withdrawal of the small number of American forces still stationed on the island. The United States did, however, reassert its interest in a peaceful future for Taiwan and continued to sell a rather sizable quantity of defensive arms to the island.

Having made these gains with regard to Taiwan, the PRC then shifted its attention to Hong Kong for the first time since 1949. The impending expiration of the lease to the New Territories in 1997 compelled London to seek an agreement with Beijing over Hong Kong's future. When talks between the two governments began in 1982, London's initial proposal was to maintain British administration over the entire territory for an indefinite period after the lease to the New Territories lapsed. But this proposal proved unacceptable to Beijing, which steadfastly insisted upon the reassertion of Chinese sovereignty over Hong Kong once the present arrangements came to an end.

After long and difficult negotiations, Britain and China reached an agreement on the future of Hong Kong in September 1984. In the end, the joint statement issued by the two governments was more flexible, binding, and forthcoming than any observers had expected would be possible. In essence, it provided that Hong Kong would, after 1997, become a "special administrative region" of the People's Republic of China, with a "high degree of autonomy" in all matters except for defense and foreign affairs. It specified the distinctive features of Hong Kong's present administrative, legal, economic, educational, and social systems, and pledged that all of them would be preserved for at least 50 years after the reassertion of Chinese sovereignty. This notion of a capitalist Hong Kong existing inside a socialist China was summarized by Beijing in the formula "one country, two systems."

Nevertheless, China has also insisted on some provisions that symbolize the fact that Hong Kong will not become an independent entity, but rather a local jurisdiction under the central Chinese government. Despite some reservations in Hong Kong, Beijing has reserved the prerogative to station troops in the territory as a symbol of its sovereignty. The Sino-British agreement also stipulates that China will have the right to appoint Hong Kong's chief executive, adopt (and presumably to amend) the Basic Law, or mini-constitution, of the Hong Kong special administrative region, and overturn any local legislation that is in conflict with the Basic Law. And on several occasions, Deng Xiaoping has said that Beijing might well interfere in the affairs of Hong Kong if Chinese leaders were to conclude that this would be in the territory's best interests.

The terms of the agreement with Britain reflect Beijing's two major interests in Hong Kong. First, China wants Hong Kong to remain stable and prosperous. A flourishing Hong Kong can make an enormous contribution to the modernization of southeast China by serving as a source of capital, technology, information, and managerial talent. Similarly, continued economic prosperity and political stability in Hong Kong after 1997 will make reunification a more attractive proposition for the people of Taiwan. Conversely, a Hong Kong suffering from serious economic and social dislocations could only be a drain on scarce Chinese resources, an embarrassment to Beijing internationally, and a virtual guarantee that Taiwan would never agree to reunification with the mainland. Beijing recognizes, moreover, that the best way to maintain the stability and prosperity of Hong Kong is to offer the territory a high degree of local autonomy

42

and to pledge to preserve its present social and economic system for a protracted period after 1997.

At the same time, however, Beijing also wishes to secure control over the broad course of events in Hong Kong, so as to maximize the benefits from the territory and to minimize the probability of untoward developments. At present, it appears that the Chinese will do so through a combination of official and unofficial channels. Officially, the process of the appointment of the chief executive and the confirmation of local legislation will give Beijing some power over the decisions of local government. Unofficially, Beijing will also attempt to gain influence by increasing its economic investment in Hong Kong, by maintaining informal contacts with the territory's economic and social elites, by reinforcing its ties to major newspapers and trade unions, and by maintaining a small Communist Party network in Hong Kong. The challenge for Beijing is to build and exercise this leverage in ways that do not destroy local confidence in the relative autonomy of Hong Kong's political system.

From Beijing's perspective, these two somewhat contradictory goals can best be achieved if there is relatively little change in the political system that existed in 1984: an non-elected chief executive, a weak appointed legislature, and an absence of organized political parties. The PRC fears that movement toward full pluralistic democracy in Hong Kong would run the risk of social disorder and economic instability. It might also produce decisions that would be unacceptable to Beijing, forcing the central government to face the unpalatable choice between grudging acquiescence and formal disapproval.

As we will see in the next chapter, however, some vocal groups in Hong Kong find the perpetuation of the present form of local government to be unacceptable. As they see it, true autonomy requires real democracy, including a strong legislature directly elected by its constituents through a process that involves competing political parties. China has resisted such proposals. Chinese officials responsible for Hong Kong affairs have acknowledged that there should be a more even balance of power between the executive and the legislature. But they have not accepted a multiparty electoral system and have warned that the Chinese Communist Party would be required to take a much more active role in Hong Kong were other political parties to be formed. Nor are they enthusiastic about the use of direct elections to select members of the legislature.

The Sino-British agreement on Hong Kong has served as the model for the future of the Portuguese territory of Macao. In March 1987, Portugal and China initialed a joint statement that closely parallels the earlier document on Hong Kong and that often uses the same terminology. Like Hong Kong, Macao will become a special administrative region of China, with a "high degree of autonomy" in its internal affairs and with the right to maintain its present social and economic systems for at least 50 years. Portugal had sought, unsuccessfully, to delay the transfer of sovereignty over Macao until sometime early in the 21st century. Instead, at Chinese insistence, the Portuguese flag will be drawn down on December 20, 1999—two and a half years after Hong Kong becomes Chinese, but a few days short of the new century. Portugal was more successful in gaining passages in the agreement that guarantee legal rights and employment opportunities for those of Portuguese descent who choose to remain in Macao.

Beijing would also like to apply the concept of "one country, two systems" to Taiwan. Indeed, Chinese officials have indicated that Beijing will be even more flexible in applying this formula to Taiwan than it was in its negotiations with the British and the Portuguese. China has said that, after unification, Taiwan would be able to maintain its own armed forces and its own political parties and that representatives of the Kuomintang would be given positions in the central government in Beijing. Deng Xiaoping has also pledged that no military or administrative personnel from the mainland would be stationed on Taiwan. But Beijing continues to rule out any formulas that would not clearly acknowledge Taiwan to be under the jurisdiction of the People's Republic of China. Thus, Chinese spokesmen have rejected the application of the "German model" to Taiwan, under which the island would be recognized as a separate country within a broader entity known as the Chinese nation. Similarly, Chinese officials have shown no interest in changing the present unitary system of government in the PRC to a federal or confederal form as a way of guaranteeing greater autonomy for Taiwan.

Beijing also adamantly refuses to renounce the use of force against Taiwan, on the grounds that doing so would eliminate many of the incentives for the government of Taiwan to negotiate and would simultaneously remove one of the principal disincentives against a unilateral declaration of independence by the Taiwanese. Indeed, some Chinese leaders have expressed their desire to develop the capability to blockade Taiwan in the event that some form of military pressure against the island should become desirable.

On the other hand, China has frequently reiterated its preference for the peaceful reunification of Taiwan and the mainland, agreeing to include a statement to this effect in the 1982 agreement with the United States on the reduction of American arms sales to Taiwan. It has withdrawn many of the forces that were once stationed along the

Taiwan Straits and has stopped its symbolic bombardment of the offshore islands. Moreover, Beijing has specified a rather limited set of conditions under which it would use force against Taiwan. These include the development of nuclear weapons by Taiwan, a unilateral declaration of independence by the Taiwanese government, a strategic alignment between Taipei and the Soviet Union, serious political instability in Taiwan, or a "protracted refusal to negotiate" with the mainland. In so doing, Beijing has strongly implied that it would refrain from the use of force under any other set of circumstances.

In assessing the prospects for Taiwan's future, Beijing is faced with a dilemma. In the past, it has placed its hopes on negotiations with the mainlanders who still dominate the Kuomintang, in the belief that these men retain the greatest commitment to the concept of "one China." But Beijing has slowly come to realize the difficulties with such an approach. For one thing, the elders of the Kuomintang are adamantly opposed to negotiations with the Communists. For another, the mainlanders on Taiwan would face serious domestic opposition if they were to attempt to discuss the island's future with their counterparts in Beijing, for the Taiwanese community would suspect that its interests would be sacrificed in the process. Furthermore, the aging mainlanders are slowly passing from the political scene, and Taiwanese representatives are gradually gaining more prominence in their own political system.

In recent months, therefore, Beijing has begun to pay greater attention to this younger generation of Taiwanese, both inside and outside the Kuomintang, who will become increasingly influential in the years ahead. Some Chinese analysts have begun to speak of the need to establish contacts with the "Taiwanese people," including politicians active in the island's opposition movement. But they have also begun to express their concern about the resurgence of a Taiwan independence movement and the possibility that it might gain supporters in the United States. Chinese analysts have noted with some disquiet the emergence of a new opposition party on Taiwan, the Democratic Progressive Party, whose platform calls for "self-determination" for the island—very possibly a veiled reference to independence.

Although there is a growing realization in Beijing that reunification with Taiwan must be a gradual and protracted process, China will remain alert to any signs that this ultimate goal is becoming more elusive. Thus, the PRC can be expected to react quickly and sharply to the development of a strong Taiwan independence movement, either in third countries or on the island itself. China will also object, as it has in the past, to any indications that either the United States or

Japan is retreating from past commitments on the Taiwan issue. Of particular concern would be an increase in the quantity or sophistication of American arms sold to the island, support for "self-determination" or independence for Taiwan, or an attempt to restore officiality to American or Japanese relations with Taipei.

In addition, if Beijing's patience on the Taiwan issue wears thin, there is the strong possibility that it will attempt to persuade the United States to force Taipei to negotiate. Already, Chinese officials have asked the United States to take a more active role in promoting the unification of Taiwan and the mainland. Ideally, they would like to see the repeal of the Taiwan Relations Act, which provides the legal framework for the sale of arms to the island and embodies the American commitment to a peaceful future for Taiwan. China has also pressed for a more rapid reduction in American arms sales to Taiwan, American endorsement of the "one country, two systems" formula, and American support for the establishment of trade, postal service, and communications links between Taiwan and the mainland. Thus far, Beijing has placed only limited weight behind these demands. But if China should decide that the trends in Taiwan were running in directions unfavorable to reunification, it might very well decide to increase the pressure on the United States.

Even so, the connection between the Hong Kong and Taiwan issues will continue to put significant constraints on China, at least through 1997. If China does not show continued flexibility in drafting the Basic Law for Hong Kong, and if it does not show restraint in its comments on Hong Kong's internal affairs, then the attractiveness of the Hong Kong formula for Taiwan will be that much reduced. Conversely, if China placed considerable political pressure on either Taiwan or the United States between now and 1997, or if it decided to use any kind of military force against Taipei, then it could only expect the rapid hemorrhage of capital and people from Hong Kong as the 1997 deadline approaches.

IV. Northeast Asia Looks at China

As already noted, the countries of Northeast Asia regard contemporary China with considerable ambivalence. Most of them agree that China has entered an era in its foreign relations that is more constructive than any other since the establishment of the People's Republic in 1949. Both publicly and privately, officials and intellectuals in Northeast Asian capitals express satisfaction with the main features of Beijing's present international orientation, particularly its emphasis on economic modernization, its desire for a peaceful international environment, its growing pragmatism and flexibility, and its increasing support for the international political and economic order.

As they look toward the future, however, many of these same observers view China with greater concern, verging in some cases on alarm. Many Northeast Asians are firmly convinced that, given the opportunity, Beijing will attempt to reassert its traditional cultural and political supremacy over the rest of the region. Many are troubled by the fact that China has some sort of unresolved territorial dispute with every one of its Northeast Asian neighbors: disagreements over its land borders with the Soviet Union and North Korea, controversies over maritime boundaries and resources with South Korea and Japan, an alleged desire to reincorporate Mongolia into a larger Chinese state, and the acknowledged goal of achieving the reunification of Taiwan with the Chinese mainland. Moreover, many Northeast Asians fear that Beijing's current program of sustained modernization will, for the first time in centuries, give China formidable material resources, both economic and military, with which to pursue these goals of political hegemony, territorial integrity, and national unity.

The prevailing perceptions of China in Northeast Asia are similar to those held by the nations to the south of China. In both parts of Asia, there is a common conviction that, once it becomes strong, China will attempt to reestablish its historical role as the center of Asian culture and politics. The territorial issues that trouble China's relations with its Northeast Asian neighbors find their parallels in the border disputes in which Beijing has long been engaged with India and Vietnam. In both Northeast and Southeast Asia, there is an understandable apprehension about the impact of sustained economic and military modernization in a country with China's population and resources.

Nonetheless, in one important respect worries about China's future course are more muted in Asia's northeast corner than in the southeastern part of the region. The large number of Overseas Chinese in Southeast Asia—particularly in Indonesia and Malaysia—is an important irritant in China's relations with those countries that has no counterpart in China's dealings with the Northeast Asian states. Overseas Chinese have played a disproportionate role in both the economic elites and the Communist parties of many Southeast Asian countries. As a result, Overseas Chinese are frequently perceived, albeit often unfairly, as a subversive force more loyal to China than to their country of residence, which Beijing can mobilize to achieve its foreign policy goals. In contrast, there are relatively few Overseas Chinese living in Japan, Korea, or the Soviet Union.

To be sure, there is also an ethnic element in China's relations with some Northeast Asian countries. Sizable ethnic groups, including Uighurs, Mongols, and Koreans, straddle China's boundaries with the Soviet Union, Mongolia, and North Korea. Occasionally, the ties that these peoples have maintained with their relatives across the borders, and even their physical movements from one side to another, have been a cause of tension in China's relations with these three neighboring states. Even so, there is a fundamental difference between the ethnic situation in Northeast Asia and that in Southeast Asia. In Northeast Asia, the ethnic issue involves not Overseas Chinese but non-Chinese peoples. It is, accordingly, more difficult for China's Northeast Asian neighbors to regard these groups as instruments of Chinese influence. Indeed, just as frequently, it has been Beijing that has seen these non-Chinese communities as a threat to its own national unity and security.

To examine Northeast Asian attitudes toward China in somewhat greater detail, it is convenient to divide the states of the region into three broad categories on the basis of the intensity of their concern about growing Chinese economic resources, military power, and political leverage. In the first group are the two large regional powers—Japan and the Soviet Union—which are reasonably pleased with Beijing's current orientation in international affairs but which see the PRC as a possible rival for influence in the more distant future. In a second group are two smaller states—North and South Korea—which, to a degree unique in Northeast Asia, see the PRC as a potential benefactor in a multipolar region, serving to counterbalance other nations which may pose even greater threats to their security. Finally, the three territories with the smallest populations—Hong Kong, Taiwan, and Mongolia—all believe themselves to be the targets of increasing Chinese irredentism and are deeply concerned about their future relationship to the mainland Chinese state.

The Regional Powers: China as Rival

In examining the prevailing attitudes toward China in the Soviet Union and Japan, we encounter the paradoxical situation that two countries with very different cultures, political systems, and international orientations still view China in somewhat similar fashion. Both Soviet and Japanese scholars and officials profess optimism about their relationships with China over the medium term, but this is largely because they interpret recent developments in China in quite different ways. The Japanese see the Chinese reforms as moving China away from its Maoist past in a more liberal direction and therefore predict that, in foreign affairs, Beijing will remain closer to the West than to the Soviet Union. Conversely, Soviet specialists predict that, when the dust of reform settles, the Chinese economic and political order will remain socialist in character and are confident that Beijing will therefore find more in common with the Soviet Union than with the West.

Although both the Soviet Union and Japan are therefore reasonably sanguine about their present relationships with China, they share a common concern that, over the longer run, Beijing's current program of economic modernization will transform China into a powerful, assertive, and disruptive military and political force in Asia. Furthermore, in contrast to the Soviet Union, there persists in Japan a sizable body of opinion that China's effort at economic reform will ultimately fail, that the PRC will descend into social and political disorder, and that this development, as much as successful modernization, will have a profoundly destabilizing effect on the rest of the region.

In Moscow, both scholars and officials express substantial gratification with recent developments in Chinese foreign policy. In particular, Soviet specialists are relieved that China has disavowed any intention to form the sort of strategic alignment with the United States that appeared imminent in the late 1970s in the wake of the normalization of Sino-American relations and the Vietnamese invasion of Cambodia. Furthermore, Soviet observers have also taken pleasure in the fact that, without any major concessions from Moscow except for a cessation of the polemics previously directed against China, Beijing was willing to significantly expand its cultural, educational, and economic relations with the Soviet Union.

49

Originally, the Soviet Union refused to make any compromises on the three problems that the Chinese had identified as the principal obstacles to the full normalization of Sino-Soviet relations. Since Beijing had agreed to the expansion of its nonpolitical ties with Moscow in the absence of any compromises by the Kremlin, Soviet policymakers had reason to hope that the Chinese would also ultimately accept the normalization of the political and diplomatic relationship between the two countries without any preconditions. Soviet spokesmen insisted that the three obstacles were simply a device by which the Chinese rationalized their hostility toward the Soviet Union. When Beijing decided it had an interest in further improvements in its relations with Moscow, they argued, it would easily find ways of setting the three obstacles aside. Soviet officials also noted that they had not established any preconditions for an improvement of their relations with China, even though they could easily identify some if they wished to, and expressed some resentment that China was attempting to win concessions from Moscow as the price for a reduction of tensions. Furthermore, Soviet observers pointed out, China was raising issues that involved Soviet relations with third countries—particularly Afghanistan, Vietnam, and Mongolia—that could not properly be linked to the bilateral relationship between Moscow and Beijing.

By early 1986, however, there was mounting evidence that China would not, in fact, agree to the normalization of its political relations with Moscow unless the Soviet Union made compromises on at least one of the three obstacles. A more open-minded group of Soviet sinologists in the Foreign Ministry and in the academic community therefore argued for, and won Gorbachev's agreement to, the concessions contained in the General Secretary's speech in Vladivostok in July of that year. This reflected a calculation that carefully chosen Soviet overtures could facilitate and accelerate the warming in relations between Beijing and Moscow.

Soviet observers have adduced several reasons for further optimism about their relations with China, at least over the middle term. They point to a number of areas in which China and the Soviet Union have taken parallel policies: opposition to the American Strategic Defense Initiative (SDI), renunciation of the first use of nuclear weapons, criticism of the American involvement in Central America, denunciation of American raids against Libya, rejection of the American position on South Africa, and so forth. They anticipate growing tensions between China and the United States over the Taiwan question, human rights, and economic issues. Conversely, they note that Moscow has consistently supported Beijing's position on Taiwan

50

and assert that the similarity between the Chinese and Soviet economies will serve to facilitate Sino-Soviet trade. Soviet spokesmen claim that, while China has been running chronic trade deficits with Japan and (to a lesser degree) with the United States, the Soviet Union can easily ensure a balance in its commercial transactions with China. Furthermore, noting Chinese concerns about "spiritual pollution" from the West, they argue that economic relations with the Soviet Union will incur absolutely no social or political domestic costs for Beijing.

In addition, Soviet observers are convinced that the political and economic systems of the two countries are engaged in a gradual process of convergence. Although views on the future of China's reforms vary, the opinion of the majority of Soviet officials and analysts is that Beijing will place strict limits on economic and political liberalization and that China will therefore remain a socialist country under Party rule. At the same time, the reform program currently being undertaken by Mikhail Gorbachev will introduce into the Soviet Union some of the same experiments with market forces, private entrepreneurship, and foreign investment that have characterized the Chinese experience under Deng Xiaoping. Soviet specialists emphasize the fact that each country is now prepared to acknowledge the other to be a socialist state. And, as one Soviet scholar has put it, the fact that China and the Soviet Union maintain a common commitment to socialism is an "objective guarantee" of a relatively warm and cooperative Sino-Soviet relationship.

Just beneath this optimism, however, lies a much more apprehensive view of China. Many Soviet officials and intellectuals, perhaps as a result of events dating as far back as the Mongol invasion of Russia in the thirteenth century, retain a deep-seated uneasiness about Asians. The growth of the Asian population of the Soviet Union, the strategic vulnerability of Siberia, and the conviction that China still harbors designs on large amounts of Soviet territory in the Far East simply intensify their fears. For the first time, Moscow faces the prospect of a China that is politically unified, is effectively modernizing, and has close ties to the principal adversaries of the Soviet Union. This outcome is what Russian policymakers have feared for a hundred years and what they have consistently sought to prevent.

Despite their celebration of the common socialist orientation of China and the Soviet Union, therefore, many Soviet observers become more guarded when asked for their longer-term projections of China's future role in Asia. Some believe that China may yet form a strategic alignment with the United States directed against the Soviet Union. Others worry that, as it becomes stronger, China will

51

seek to expand its influence into Southeast Asia, implying that the Soviet Union would inevitably be drawn into the international alignment that would form to resist Chinese inroads. Asked about his view of China's emergence as a major military power, one leading Soviet commentator, who had just concluded a relatively sanguine analysis of the current state of Sino-Soviet relations, acknowledged that Moscow "would not be jubilant about such a development."

Much the same combination of satisfaction with the present and uneasiness about the future that one finds in the Soviet Union is also evident in Japanese images of China. Japanese observers regard the present stage in Chinese foreign policy as the most favorable to Japanese interests since 1949. China is, today, a stabilizing force in Korea. It is no longer closely aligned with the Soviet Union, and its armed forces offer a counterweight to the Soviet military presence in Siberia. It has supported the Japanese claim to the small islands just north of Hokkaido that are occupied by the Soviet Union. Beijing is no longer opposed to Japan's Mutual Security Treaty with the United States and expresses its understanding of the gradual development of Japan's military capability. Above all, China offers significant economic opportunities to Japanese traders and investors.

Looking toward the future, however, Japanese observers—like their Soviet counterparts—are much more ambivalent. In large part this ambivalence is due to the long and complex historical relationship between China and Japan. Japan borrowed much from China in the seventh and eighth centuries—schools of philosophy, styles of painting, a system of writing, and a form of government. The teacher-student relationship between the two societies was reversed in the late nineteenth century, however, when the Meiji Restoration in Japan provided a more effective response to the challenge of the West than did the contemporaneous Tongzhi Restoration in China. Thereafter, it was Chinese intellectuals who turned to Japan for information about modern science, industry, and politics. But the gap between the two countries still widened, and, by the beginning of the twentieth century, Japan had launched a policy of economic penetration and political influence in China that culminated in an all-out military invasion in the late 1930s.

This complicated historical relationship with China has produced an amalgam of attitudes in Japan, blending admiration for China's traditional culture, contempt for China's modern weakness, guilt for Japan's behavior toward China between 1895 and 1945, and even fear of how China might seek restitution for past Japanese aggression. Perhaps in consequence, there is a wider range of views about China's future in Japan than anywhere else in Northeast Asia.

One nightmare, common among a certain segment of Japanese intellectuals, is of China in collapse. This draws on the images, prevalent in the early twentieth century, of a China that was culturally and politically unable to modernize effectively and that was plagued by an insoluble contradiction between a huge population and limited arable land. More recent episodes in Chinese history—including the Great Leap Forward, the Cultural Revolution, and the economic retrenchments of the post-Mao period—are cited to show that China still has not been able to construct a political structure or devise an economic strategy that can produce sustained modernization. Tensions in the current reform program—protests, corruption, and inflation—are also used to support the argument that the Chinese political, social, and economic scene remains highly unstable.

Japanese pessimists further argue that the collapse of reform in China would be a dangerously destabilizing development for the rest of Asia. Some Japanese accept the argument that it was the instability on the Chinese mainland in the 1920s and 1930s that ineluctably drew Japan into increasing involvement in Chinese affairs. Using a similar logic, they assert that instability in China today would also produce a vacuum into which the major powers, including the United States and the Soviet Union, would unavoidably be drawn. Virtually alone in Asia, it is this school of thought in Japan that expresses the worry that, in the future, China will be a disruptive force in the region by being too weak.

As China moves further from the Maoist era, however, this pessimistic school appears to be steadily losing strength. Rather than forecasting a China in collapse, the majority of Japanese foresee a China that will modernize, albeit through a process that is slow, painful, and halting. Increasingly prevalent in Japan is the viewpoint, common in most of the rest of Asia, that modernization in China may in fact succeed but that it will jeopardize the security of the rest of the region.

The specific scenarios implied by a powerful China vary from observer to observer. Some Japanese are concerned with the development of Chinese military power, particularly with the emergence of a modern bluewater navy. Some still fear the renewal of a Sino-Soviet alliance, directed against both Japan and the United States. Others worry about a deterioration in Sino-American relations, with Japan caught awkwardly between Washington and Beijing, as it was through much of the 1950s and 1960s. Still others express a more general suspicion that China will seek to exclude Japanese influence from the rest of Asia and restrict Japan to a peripheral role in regional affairs.

Given these apprehensions, Japanese observers were troubled by the tensions that began to emerge in their relations with China between 1985 and 1987. Like the United States in the early 1980s, Japan experienced a steady drumbeat of complaints from the Chinese over a wide range of issues: the alleged resurgence of Japanese militarism, the increases in the Japanese defense budget, the ties between Japan and Taiwan, the chronic imbalances in Sino-Japanese trade, and the reluctance of Japanese corporations to make large investments in China. The sudden and unexpected dismissal of Hu Yaobang, who was widely regarded in Tokyo as the Chinese leader most sympathetic to Japan, was particularly troubling to Japanese analysts. They were disturbed by the evidence that Hu's favorable attitudes toward Japan may have played a role, however small, in igniting the political crisis that culminated in his resignation in January 1987.

In short, there is growing disquietude in Japan with the specter of a powerful, unified, and modern China. As one perceptive Japanese intellectual has pointed out, the Japanese government, unlike its American counterpart, has never expressed a desire to see a "strong China." Instead, Tokyo's interest is in a "stable and slowly modernizing China." The temporal element in this formulation is revealing, in that it suggests the way in which many Japanese observers try to resolve the contradiction between their satisfaction with the present course of Chinese policy and their uneasiness about the future. The Japanese hope that the process of modernization in China will be so protracted that Japan will be able to reap the benefits of this orientation while avoiding the risks attendant upon its fulfillment for a long time to come. In the words of one prominent Japanese sinologist: "We Japanese hope that China will continue to devote all its energies to the task of modernization. We also hope that it will never succeed."

The Smaller Powers: China as Counterweight

In light of the bitter confrontation between the two Koreas, it is ironic that the perceptions of the PRC held in Pyongyang and Seoul are remarkably similar. In some ways, each of the two Koreas sees Beijing as a potential source of support in its struggle with its rival. Pyongyang can point to China's involvement in the Korean War, the DPRK's current military alliance with the PRC, and Beijing's endorsement of most of North Korea's diplomatic initiatives toward the United States and South Korea. For its part, South Korea can reasonably regard its burgeoning informal political and economic contacts with Beijing, together with China's oft-stated desire for continued stability on the Korean peninsula, as evidence that the PRC serves as a restraint against North Korean adventurism.

Moreover, neither Korea regards China as a direct threat to its own security. North Korea is concerned with what it believes to be the challenge posed by the United States and Japan, while South Korea is worried more by the intentions of North Korea, the Soviet Union, and even Japan than it is by China. Indeed, both Pyongyang and Seoul appear to perceive the PRC as a welcome addition to the major power constellation surrounding them, hoping that Beijing will serve as a counterweight to those nations that pose a greater threat to their security.

Although the image of China held in both Pyongyang and Seoul is thus basically positive, neither Korea can be absolutely certain that Beijing will, in the final analysis, remain completely reliable. Seoul fears that China's past commitments to the DPRK, as well as its continuing rivalry with the Soviet Union for influence in Pyongyang, would force Beijing to choose the North over the South in any crisis on the Korean peninsula. In the same way, Pyongyang probably regards Beijing's obvious flirtation with Seoul as a sign of Chinese infidelity and may assume that China's growing ties with the United States would prevent it from giving wholehearted support to the North in the event of renewed hostilities.

Of the two Koreas, it is the North that best maintains the country's traditional reputation as a "Hermit Kingdom," isolated from the rest of the world. The lack of contact between North Korea and the United States—and the apparent lack of intimacy between North Korea and its two Communist allies—makes it difficult to know with certainty much about Pyongyang's views of China. Nevertheless, it is possible to speculate about North Korean attitudes toward the PRC in a reasonably informed manner.

For most of the past four decades, North Korea has considered China to be a more generous and less overbearing partner than the Soviet Union. To be sure, as a country whose per capita income is actually lower than that of North Korea, China has had less to offer the DPRK in the way of advanced weaponry, technical assistance, or economic support than has the Soviet Union. Indeed, on virtually every material dimension—trade, military equipment, and financial aid—Moscow has given more to North Korea than has Beijing. Nonetheless, Beijing has been forthcoming in other ways. It was China, not the Soviet Union, that sent troops to fight alongside the North Korean armies during the Korean conflict. The Soviet Union was, during the 1960s and 1970s, notably reluctant to transfer top-of-the-line military equipment to the North Korean armed forces. Unlike China, the Soviet Union has not acknowledged the DPRK as the "sole legal government" on the Korean peninsula. And the Soviet Union has assigned much lower priority to the Korean question in its foreign policy than has the PRC.

Conversely, the Soviet Union has occasionally attempted to exercise influence over North Korea's internal affairs. Indeed, in the mid-1950s a group of dissidents within the North Korean elite attempted to dislodge Kim Il-sung from leadership, or at least to seriously weaken his position. In this the dissidents were apparently inspired by Khrushchev's attack in 1956 on the "cult of personality" surrounding Stalin, and they may well have received direct Soviet assistance and support. Although the attempt failed, Kim Il-sung has seen it necessary to wage a continuing struggle to preserve his autonomy from Soviet control.

Because of these considerations, North Korea has generally tilted more toward Beijing than toward Moscow, although it has simultaneously worked to preserve reasonably friendly relations with the Soviet Union. In the late 1970s, for example, Pyongyang echoed many of Beijing's complaints about Soviet "social-imperialism," although it used the somewhat softer term, "dominationism," as its code word in describing Soviet conduct in international affairs. North Korea's relations with two of the Soviet Union's closest allies, Vietnam and Cuba, were seriously strained, and Kim Il-sung offered a palatial residence to Prince Norodom Sihanouk while the exiled Cambodian leader sought to mobilize international resistance to the Vietnamese invasion of his country.

More recently, however, North Korea has grown increasingly suspicious of Chinese policy and intentions. Pyongyang has been concerned about Beijing's interest in developing unofficial relations with Seoul, particularly in the economic realm. The DPRK must be irritated by the fact that, by the mid-1980s, China's trade with South Korea exceeded by a substantial margin its trade with the North and by the fact that much of it is now carried on ships that travel directly between the two countries. By protesting to Beijing, Pyongyang has been able to limit China's relations with Seoul and, on occasion, has even forced temporary reductions in the PRC's trade with South Korea. Even so, it is clear to the North that China would like to develop its ties with Seoul to the greatest extent possible. This suggests to Pyongyang that Beijing would prefer to institutionalize the status quo on the peninsula rather than actively to promote Korean reunification on the North's terms.

As a result, North Korea has, in the last several years, moved toward a warmer relationship with the Soviet Union and has adopted a roughly equidistant posture between Beijing and Moscow. The Soviet Union has reciprocated North Korean goodwill by acknowledging Kim Jong-il as his father's successor, increasing its economic assistance to Pyongyang, and finally supplying the North Korean air force with the MiG-23 fighters it has so long desired. The price imposed by Moscow has not been inconsiderable. The Kremlin has secured permission for Soviet aircraft to fly through North Korean airspace en route to their reconnaissance missions along the Chinese coast and the right for ships of the Soviet navy to call at North Korean ports. Even so, Pyongyang has apparently been willing to accept these conditions as a way of signaling its dissatisfaction with Chinese policies toward Seoul.

A further cause for North Korean dissatisfaction was China's inability to persuade the United States to be more flexible in its policy toward Korea. In 1983, Beijing encouraged North Korea to accept an American proposal, originally put forward by the Carter administration, for tripartite talks among the United States and the two Koreas. But the details of Pyongyang's acceptance, coupled with the fact that it occurred simultaneously with the attempted assassination of the South Korean cabinet in Rangoon, caused the Reagan administration to reject the North Korean overtures. Ultimately, in early 1987, the United States did agree to a very limited diplomatic dialogue with North Korea and offered to make further concessions if Pyongyang responded with positive gestures of its own. The fact that Washington relayed this message through Beijing and that the American initiatives were made at China's urging may have helped improve China's standing in North Korean eyes.

Like Pyongyang, Seoul is keenly aware of Beijing's desire to expand the unofficial relations between China and South Korea. But where Pyongyang seeks to limit those ties, Seoul wants to encourage them. Thus visiting delegations from China are treated lavishly, and South Korean teams participating in international sporting events in China are given considerable coverage in the South Korean press.

Seoul's hope, of course, is to woo China away from an exclusive relationship with North Korea. It has been gratified by the increase in its trade with the PRC, by China's obvious interest in preserving peace along the DMZ, and by Beijing's decision to send large delegations to Seoul to attend the Asian Games in 1986 and the Olympics in 1988. The South Koreans hope that, over time, China will move even closer to Seoul's position on a number of key issues. Ideally, from the South Korean perspective, Beijing ultimately will participate (along with Washington, Pyongyang, and Seoul) in quadripartite talks on the Korean question, support the admission of both Koreas to the United Nations, and even agree to establish formal diplomatic relations with both Korean regimes.

South Korea's competition with the North aside, Seoul also has other motives for improving its relations with China. Like the other East Asian NICs, South Korea perceives a considerable economic opportunity in a growing China market. Although they lack the ethnic ties to China that are enjoyed by Singapore, Hong Kong, and Taiwan, the Koreans have certain other advantages. South Korea has, of all the NICs, the most highly developed heavy-industry sector, and it is in close proximity to the Chinese industrial base in Manchuria. This suggests the possibility of exchanging Korean capital equipment and consumer goods for Chinese oil, coal, and other natural resources.

Despite this optimistic assessment of their future relations with China, South Korean scholars and officials still have lingering suspicions about the implications of China's long-standing relationship with North Korea. In particular, they believe that one of Pyongyang's principal strategic objectives is to develop the capability to launch a surprise attack against the South without gaining the prior consent of either Beijing or Moscow. In such a circumstance, South Korean strategists worry, the Chinese might feel compelled to honor their alliance with Pyongyang and provide military and economic assistance to the DPRK. What is more, even short of such an extreme scenario, South Korean military planners are concerned about the transfer of American military technology to the PRC, on the grounds that some of it might, intentionally or not, fall into North Korean hands.

These reservations notwithstanding, what is striking is that of all the non-Communist states in Asia South Korea's attitudes toward China are by far the most positive. To a degree, this reflects the fact that Korea regards its historical ties to China more favorably than do many other recipients of Sinitic cultural influence. Indeed, South Korean intellectuals not only point out the importance of Confucianism in Korean culture but also occasionally argue that South Korea, which has been free from Communist rule or cultural revolutions, has remained more loyal to its Confucian roots than even China itself. Equally important, Korean sympathy toward China can also be traced to the fact that it is Japan, not China, that is Korea's traditional enemy. While Koreans recall with approval the history of their relationship with China, they have much more bitter memories of their ties with Japan: the invasion by Japanese forces in the sixteenth century (when Chinese forces came to Korea's aid), the harsh colonial rule imposed by Tokyo from 1905 to 1945, and the more recent penetration (and, some Koreans believe, exploitation) of the Korean economy by Japanese industry. In consequence, it may not be surprising that some South Korean intellectuals have said privately that they hope that China will over time modernize itself successfully so that it can serve as a counterbalance to Japanese influence in Northeast Asia.

The Weakest Territories: China as Irredentist

Three of the remaining parts of Northeast Asia—Hong Kong, Taiwan, and Mongolia—express the greatest anxiety about China's long-term intentions and capabilities, for each of them perceives itself to be a target of Chinese irredentism. The British have already agreed to return Hong Kong to Chinese sovereignty in 1997. In Taipei, there remains the fear that an impatient China might use military force or political pressure to force reunification on its own terms. And in Ulan Bator, there is a deeply held conviction that, despite official denials to the contrary, Beijing still hopes to add the two million Mongols living in Outer Mongolia to the three and a half million Mongols inside the PRC. As a result, all three of these territories look outside for some kind of protection against Chinese irredentism: Hong Kong (still) to Britain, Taiwan to the United States, and Mongolia to the Soviet Union.

On the other hand, there is also a modicum of optimism within each place. In Hong Kong, there remains the hope that economic imperatives will lead China to act with responsibility, flexibility, and restraint as the 1997 deadline approaches and the hope that an effective representative local government can be created that can enjoy legal guarantees of a high degree of autonomy from Chinese control. In Taiwan, there is also the hope, although not universally shared, that some kind of accommodation can ultimately be reached with a more prosperous and liberalized mainland regime, albeit not necessarily a settlement that would acknowledge Beijing's legal jurisdiction over the island. Even in Ulan Bator, there is recognition that the recent improvements in Sino-Soviet relations may well be accompanied by a relaxation in tensions between China and Mongolia.

In Hong Kong, there is now a general consensus that Beijing genuinely wishes to maintain economic prosperity and social stability in the territory after the transition to Chinese sovereignty in 1997.

There is, in addition, a relatively high degree of satisfaction with the terms of the agreement on Hong Kong's future that was reached by China and Great Britain in 1984. These optimistic assessments are, however, tempered by more sobering calculations about the future. There is a widespread fear that Beijing will not exercise enough restraint between now and then to make life in a post-British Hong Kong attractive to the territory's professional and economic elites. Instead, many residents believe that China will attempt to exercise so much control over Hong Kong and will show so little sensitivity to the desires of the people of the city that there will be a hemorrhage of talent and capital as 1997 nears. What is more, as Hong Kongers frequently point out, the Chinese government that negotiated the 1984 agreement will not be the government that will have to implement it. And there is no guarantee that the Chinese authorities who will assume sovereignty over Hong Kong in 1997 will be as flexible and forthcoming as their predecessors.

In 1986, these general concerns were reflected in two particular issues. The most immediate question was the future of a large nuclear power plant, involving investment from both China and Hong Kong, that is planned for construction at Daya Bay, in Chinese territory just outside Hong Kong. In the wake of the disaster at Chernobyl, one million Hong Kongers—fully twenty percent of the population—signed petitions objecting to the project on the grounds that the safety of the plant was uncertain. But the issue soon took on political overtones, as one Chinese representative dismissed the activists as "a bunch of amateur politicians trying to take advantage of schoolchildren and the gullible man-in-the-street,"[14] and as Chinese Premier Zhao Ziyang refused to meet with a delegation sent from Hong Kong to discuss the issue. Many Hong Kong residents believed such actions to reflect the tendency of Chinese officials to disregard Hong Kong opinion, even on issues of great concern to the territory.

The second and related issue concerned the political system that will be put in place in Hong Kong as part of the 1984 agreement. The Chinese have accepted the basic principles that there will be a legislative assembly produced by elections, that the governor will be appointed by Beijing after some form of "consultation or election" in Hong Kong, and that the local administration will be "accountable" to the Hong Kong legislature. But despite this agreement on the broad outlines of Hong Kong's future political structure, many ambiguities remain. Will there be direct elections to the legislature, with competition among formally organized political parties? Or will the elections, as in today's China, be indirect and essentially noncompetitive?

14Agence France Presse, July 18, 1986, in FBIS, July 21, 1986, pp. K1-2.

How much voice will the people of Hong Kong have in the selection of their chief executive? Will the legislature be little more than an advisory body, or will it have the power to reject legislation, determine expenditures, and even express a lack of confidence in the executive? Above all, will Beijing have the right to overturn executive decisions and legislative actions taken in Hong Kong after 1997? Or will Hong Kong indeed have virtually complete autonomy in local affairs?

It is clear that the Chinese do not wish there to be any significant liberalization of the rather paternalistic political system that now exists in Hong Kong. They would prefer to take over the present system relatively intact, with the main difference being that the governor would be appointed by Beijing rather than by London. But such an approach is unacceptable to many younger people in Hong Kong, particularly younger professionals with high levels of education, who believe that the perpetuation of the current form of politics is inappropriate to the rapid economic and social development that Hong Kong has enjoyed over the last several decades. Moreover, they also worry that the Beijing government and its local appointees would abuse the powers now concentrated in the hands of Hong Kong's chief executive. Many would therefore like to see the creation of a Westminster-style government in Hong Kong, with a legislature able to force the resignation of the chief executive, members of the legislature produced by direct elections, and elections contested by well-organized political parties. Many also want restrictions on Beijing's ability to reject legislative and judicial decisions made in Hong Kong after 1997 and guarantees that the PRC will be unable to amend or modify the Basic Law governing Hong Kong without the territory's consent.

This is not to say that all Hong Kongers are pressing for a parliamentary form of government. Many older and wealthier Chinese, and the business community in general, are skeptical about the applicability of Western-style democracy to Hong Kong, fearing that it will produce political factionalism, social disorder, and economic profligacy. As a result, an intriguing set of cross-national coalitions have been formed over the political future of Hong Kong. Some young professionals in the territory are supported, at least to a degree, by a Conservative government in London and its representatives in Hong Kong in their desire for political reform before 1997. The Communist government in Beijing, in contrast, is joined by wealthy capitalists in Hong Kong in opposing a significant degree of political liberalization.

The controversies over political structure and over Daya Bay have increased the doubts of the people of Hong Kong over the longer-term viability of the territory. The percentage of the population that, in public opinion polls, expressed great confidence in the political future of Hong Kong fell from 23 percent in January 1985 to 11 percent in the summer of 1986. There remains the possibility that Beijing will steadfastly reject any true political liberalization and that the final terms of Hong Kong's "mini-constitution" will therefore prove unacceptable to large numbers of younger Hong Kong professionals. There could therefore be a destabilizing outflow of people and capital as 1997 approaches. On the other hand, as China learns more about Hong Kong, it is also conceivable that China will accept a measure of political reform in Hong Kong, that Beijing will develop greater self-restraint in commenting on local issues, and that viable local leaders and political institutions will begin to emerge. If so, confidence in the future of Hong Kong may revive between now and the turn of the century.

The evolution of the relationship between Hong Kong and the Chinese mainland is being watched with great attention and concern on Taiwan. The residents of the island are, of course, well aware that Beijing intends the formula for Hong Kong's future to apply, with some modifications, to Taiwan as well. As compared to Hong Kong, there is less conviction on Taiwan about China's good will. Moreover, the Nationalist government on Taiwan is, at the moment, much less inclined to negotiate with Beijing than were the British authorities in Hong Kong. Even so, there is growing hope in some quarters in Taipei that, over the very long term, some sort of accommodation with the PRC might ultimately be reached.

The official perceptions of the PRC are still very much shaped by an older generation of Nationalist officials, primarily mainlander in origin. Past experience—the memories of two abortive "united fronts" with the Communists in the 1920s and 1940s, the fate of Tibet and Shanghai after 1949, and the PRC's use of force against the offshore islands in the 1950s—has made them highly suspicious of Beijing's intentions. As the defeated side in the Chinese civil war in the 1940s, they are extremely cautious and wary, wanting to avoid losing any more than they have lost already.

Accordingly, this conservative faction discounts the current reforms on the mainland as little more than a Chinese version of Lenin's "New Economic Policy"—a temporary respite before a new wave of centralization and collectivization. They point out that the PRC has never renounced the use of force against Taiwan and warn that Beijing might attempt a blockade of the island once it has developed the means to do so. They worry that trade with the mainland would give Beijing the ability to destabilize the island's economy and that opening contacts across the Taiwan Straits would merely provide opportunities for the PRC to engage in subversion.

The conservatives thus maintain an unyielding posture toward Beijing. They support what are called the "three no's": a policy rejecting any negotiation, contact, or compromise with the PRC. They continue to hope for the eventual reintegration of China, but insist that it be under the political structure and political doctrine that currently govern Taiwan. In essence, therefore, they foresee the reunification of the mainland with Taiwan, rather than the other way around.

In contrast, some younger people on Taiwan—both mainlanders and Taiwanese, and both inside and outside the Kuomintang—view the situation somewhat differently. Their memories are not of the Nationalist's defeat in the civil war of the 1940s but rather of Taiwan's impressive economic successes in the 1960s and 1970s. They are, accordingly, much more self-assured and more willing to take risks than their older compatriots. As one has put it, "we see the Communists not as our enemies, but as our competitors." And many clearly believe that Taiwan has the wherewithal to compete with the PRC effectively. Perhaps as a result, younger people in Taiwan are more likely than their elders to acknowledge the extent and durability of the reforms on the mainland, and even to welcome them.

The younger generation in Taipei is, therefore, more supportive of a relaxation of tensions and the opening of unofficial contacts between Taiwan and the mainland. They are particularly interested in economic relations with the PRC, to gain both an attractive market for Taiwan's manufactured goods in a time of stagnant international trade and an outlet for Taiwan's burgeoning capital surplus. Younger scholars and business people are confident of their ability to avoid a dangerous degree of dependence on the Chinese market. Similarly, they are eager to open unofficial ties to the mainland in the areas of culture, education, and sports and to permit reestablishment of contact between divided families. Some members of the political opposition in Taiwan have even hinted that they would establish official contacts with the Communists if they came to power, although the agenda of such discussions is not altogether clear.

Still, relatively few residents of Taiwan, whether of mainland or Taiwanese origin, presently wish to acknowledge Beijing's sovereignty over the island. Some intellectuals have proposed the eventual creation of a "multistate system" for China, in which both the PRC and Taiwan agree that they are part of a broader Chinese nation, but accept equal status as separate political entities. Others, including leaders of the new opposition organization, the Democratic Progressive Party, have spoken of formal independence for the island. Thus far, the first formula has been rejected by Beijing and sharply criticized by conservatives within the Kuomintang, while the second has been anathema to both the Communists and the Nationalists. As controversial as such proposals are, however, their advocates are likely to become more vocal and more numerous in the years to come.

Recently, the leaders of the Kuomintang have shown somewhat greater flexibility in relations with the PRC. They have tolerated a high level of indirect trade between Taiwan and the mainland, estimated at around $1.2 billion in 1985, even though they periodically crack down on those businessmen who engage in direct commercial transactions with the PRC. They have unofficially sanctioned, and then in 1986 officially permitted, contacts between Taiwan and mainland scholars at meetings in third countries, particularly the United States and Japan. In 1984, Taiwan agreed to a formula whereby it would participate in the Los Angeles Olympics along with the PRC, with the Taiwan team representing the Olympic Committee of Taipei rather than the "Republic of China." Recently, sports officials in Taipei have even said that Taiwan intends to participate in the 1990 Asian Games in Beijing, if it is invited to do so. Moreover, Taipei has been willing to use the Olympic formula in other nonofficial international organizations, and there remains the possibility that it will also apply it to intergovernmental organizations, including the Asian Development Bank.

Of particular significance was an incident in mid-1986 involving the diversion of a Taiwan cargo jet to Guangzhou. The aircraft was hijacked by its own captain, who apparently wanted to be reunited with his father on the mainland. After initially refusing to negotiate the issue with the Communist representatives, Taipei ultimately agreed to hold discussions in Hong Kong between officials of China Airlines of Taiwan and the mainland's Civil Aviation Administration of China. The result was the aircraft's return to Taiwan, along with the two crew members who wished to return home. The outcome of the negotiations convinced many observers that it was indeed possible to hold successful discussions with Beijing's representatives on this kind of issue, and it may have helped to persuade the Kuomintang to permit greater contact between divided families.

Of all three territories under consideration here, it is Mongolia whose views of the PRC are the most hostile and suspicious. Mongols stress the fact that, during the Qing dynasty, they were forcibly incorporated into China—even though they simultaneously point out that the conquest of Mongolia therefore occurred at the hands of the Manchus rather than the Chinese. They point out that the establishment of the Mongolian People's Republic (MPR) in 1921 was never accepted by the republican government in China at the time, nor by the current Nationalist regime on Taiwan. They suspect, therefore, that despite its protestations to the contrary, Beijing would like to absorb the MPR into its territory, adding the two million Mongols now living in Outer Mongolia to the three and a half million who already live inside Chinese borders. The Mongolians insist—and Russian analysts agree—that on at least two occasions in the early 1950s, the Chinese informed the Soviet Union of their intention eventually to reestablish sovereignty over Outer Mongolia.[15] The more contemporary evidence they produce is somewhat strained— Chinese maps portraying the situation during World War II that do not show an independent Mongolia are used to support the argument that Beijing today does not accept a separate Mongolian state—but it appears nevertheless to be persuasive in Mongolian eyes.

Mongolian strategy in the face of this perceived threat from China is two-fold. First, they avidly insist upon their cultural distinctiveness from China. Visitors to Mongolia are asked, if they have also visited China, how they would compare the two. Those who note the differences between Chinese culture and that of Mongolia are warmly praised. Beyond this, Ulan Bator has turned to Moscow for military support, totaling in 1985 around 75,000 Soviet troops. In return for the Soviet military presence, which is particularly noticeable close to the Sino-Mongolian border, Mongolia has been willing to accept a substantial degree of economic integration with the Soviet Union, with around 80 percent of Mongolia's foreign trade being directed toward its northern neighbor, in contrast to the slightly more than 1 percent that was conducted with all nonsocialist countries. A further price has been a high level of symbolic integration between the two countries. Flags of the Soviet Union and Mongolia fly together on the main square of Ulan Bator; a huge portrait of Mikhail Gorbachev faces the mausoleum of Choybalsan and Suhbataar, the founders of the Mongolian Communist Party; and signboards proclaiming the unity of the Mongolian and Soviet peoples are displayed throughout the city.

This alliance with Moscow appears to be based less on enthusiasm for the Soviet presence than on an awareness that Mongolia has few other options if it is to maintain its independence from China. Ulan

[15]Thomas E. Stolper, *China, Taiwan, and the Offshore Islands* (Armonk, NY: M.E. Sharpe, 1985), pp. 142-46.

Bator echoes Soviet foreign policy on virtually every issue, from SDI to Central America, and from the Korean peninsula to nuclear testing. But there is one exception: discussions of China in Mongolia remain significantly more hostile and suspicious than those in the Soviet Union. One also senses that the Mongolians are not certain as to how long or how enthusiastically the Soviet Union will maintain its commitment to Mongolian security.

Recent developments in Sino-Soviet relations—especially Gorbachev's offer in July 1986 to withdraw a substantial portion of Soviet forces from Mongolia—must have heightened these concerns. The official Mongolian position had been that Soviet troops were in Mongolia at MPR's request and therefore that Beijing should discuss their withdrawal with Ulan Bator, not with Moscow. The Gorbachev proposal, however, implied that the issue would be discussed directly by China and the Soviet Union, over Mongolia's head. Ulan Bator's initial response was to move to improve relations with the PRC, by agreeing to a new consular agreement, reopening air routes to Beijing, and increasing its economic ties with China. But the Mongolians are also beginning to broaden their contacts beyond the Soviet Union—perhaps to Japan economically and to the United States politically—to find a partial counterweight to Moscow and Beijing. The establishment of diplomatic relations between Mongolia and the United States in early 1987 was an important milestone in this direction.

V. Implications for the United States and Japan

We noted at the beginning of this study that China is now playing a more active, more effective, and more influential role in the international relations of Northeast Asia than at any time in modern history. As we approach the end of this century, what are the prospects for China's relations with its neighbors in this important region? And, equally important, what are the implications of China's awakening for the United States?

Although no one can foretell the future with certainty, there are several trends in Chinese foreign policy that are likely to continue for the next fifteen years. First, it is highly probable that, given the protracted and complex nature of China's economic modernization, China will continue to assign the highest priority to the tasks of economic development and reform. Although there may be some twists and turns in the reform process, it is also likely that China will maintain its present orientation toward an economic system that provides some room for private entrepreneurship, allows a significant role for market forces, and emphasizes trade and investment relations with the outside world. This should mean that China will continue to seek a peaceful international environment, including stability on the Korean peninsula and tranquil relations with the Soviet Union.

Second, however, it is also likely that China—like all major powers—will remain concerned about its national security. In this regard, China will continue to view the Soviet Union as its principal strategic rival and will therefore regard with suspicion any attempts by Moscow to expand its political influence in Northeast Asia or to augment its already impressive military arsenal in the region. At the same time, China will also be troubled by the rise of Japanese nationalism, the strengthening of the Japanese armed forces, or the extension of Japanese security commitments beyond those Tokyo has already undertaken. Although Beijing will assign a relatively low priority to its own military modernization, it will persist in a gradual but deliberate program to upgrade the training and equipment of its armed forces.

Third, Beijing will continue to place considerable emphasis on the reunification of Hong Kong, Macao, and Taiwan with the rest of China. Given its interests in a peaceful international environment and its desire to maximize the benefits of closer economic ties with all three of these territories, Beijing's approach to the question of reunification will remain flexible and pragmatic. On the other hand, China can also be expected to react harshly to any signs that political forces in either Taipei, Tokyo, or Washington are attempting to promote an independent Taiwan. And Beijing may also decide to raise the Taiwan issue to a more prominent place in Sino-American relations if it concludes that the process of reunification is proceeding too slowly.

Finally, as the process of modernization and reform unfolds, China's economic power, political influence, and military strength will all increase. It is unlikely in the foreseeable future that these resources will be used to support an aggressive, expansionist policy characteristic of imperial powers in the past. Instead, China will use its growing power to ensure its involvement in the solution of regional issues and to obtain access to the foreign markets, capital, and technology needed for its own modernization. Still, given China's vast size, the country's awakening is likely to cause apprehension among Beijing's smaller neighbors.

Implications for the United States

These developments imply that, in the years ahead, the United States and China will share common interests on some subjects but have divergent perspectives on others, much as they do today. On balance, however, the commonalites should continue to outweigh the differences. This important fact will make it increasingly possible for the two countries to act in a parallel or collaborative fashion on those issues in which they have similar objectives, and to manage their remaining differences in a mature and responsible manner. If this can be done, then Sino-American relations may well enter a new stage, featuring growing trust and cooperation.

As they have been for nearly two decades, both China and the United States remain concerned by the expansion of Soviet military power in Northeast Asia and by the Kremlin's efforts to increase its political influence around China's periphery. Both Washington and Beijing agree on the necessity of resisting Soviet efforts to encircle China diplomatically or militarily and on the corresponding need for the United States to remain actively involved in maintaining the balance of power in Northeast Asia. Although both countries are encouraged by the recent tendencies toward reform in the Soviet Union, neither capital has yet seen signs of any fundamental change in Soviet goals or strategies in the Asia-Pacific region. Through a continuing dialogue between Chinese and American diplomatic officials and an expanding program of exchanges between their respective military establishments, the two nations have laid the groundwork for cooperation—either open or tacit—in resisting further Soviet initiatives in Asia that challenge their common interests.

Beyond this, neither China nor the United States has an interest in seeing the other enter into a more hostile relationship with the Soviet Union. From the American perspective, a significant deterioration in Sino-Soviet relations would increase the risk that the United States might be drawn into a conflict between them and would reduce the prospects for the successful management of regional disputes in East Asia, especially on the Korean peninsula. From Beijing's point of view, Chinese security would inevitably be threatened by an increase in Soviet-American tensions in Northeast Asia, particularly if it led to further reinforcement of Soviet military deployments in Siberia.

Despite these common perceptions, there remain potential differences between Beijing and Washington over their mutual relations with Moscow. Although neither country would presently favor an intensification of the other's conflict with the Soviet Union, it is also true that each side would be disturbed should the other dramatically improve its relations with the Kremlin, especially if such an accommodation occurred at the expense of its own interests.

Thus, the PRC has expressed its disapproval of any Soviet-American agreement on intermediate-range nuclear forces that would dismantle all the SS-20s presently located in Europe but would permit Moscow to deploy in Asia a smaller number of missiles targeted against China. Beijing would also be angered if the United States were to endorse a settlement of the Afghan or Cambodian conflicts that ignored Chinese interests, particularly if Washington were to accept a continuing Vietnamese presence in Cambodia while insisting on the exclusion of the Khmer Rouge. For its part, the United States would understandably object to any rapprochement between China and the Soviet Union in which Beijing dropped its objections to present Soviet policies in Asia or which permitted the Soviet Union to transfer large numbers of nuclear or conventional forces from Siberia to the European theater. It would also disapprove of the resumption of military cooperation between China and the Soviet Union or the coordination of Chinese and Soviet diplomatic initiatives in ways that were inimical to American interests.

This analysis suggests that the United States should indicate to Beijing that it has no objection in principle to a reduction of tensions between China and the Soviet Union. We would be concerned only in the unlikely event that Beijing should decide to accept or ignore the Soviet drive to expand its political influence and military presence in

Asia or should agree to engage in strategic or diplomatic cooperation with the Soviet Union that was directed against the United States. In contrast, we would welcome a Sino-Soviet accommodation that resulted from a fundamental shift in Soviet policies in Afghanistan and Cambodia or from a reduction in Soviet deployments in Siberia and Mongolia. Indeed, such a development would certainly contribute to a significant lessening of Soviet-American tensions as well.

The United States should also continue to support China's efforts to undertake a measured program of military modernization to bolster its own security against possible threats from the Soviet Union. It is in our interest to maintain and gradually expand our present policy of limited military cooperation with the PRC, involving the sale of a reasonable amount of defensive weapons to China, sharing of intelligence on Soviet capabilities and intentions, and frequent contracts between the military establishments of our two countries. We should, however, impress upon Beijing that the rapid development of China's projective military capabilities—whether ground, naval, or air— would complicate its relations with a large number of its neighbors in both Northeast and Southeast Asia, and therefore with the United States as well.

In return for our support of, and cooperation with, China's own military modernization, we should also request that China support the reasonable efforts undertaken by the United States and Japan to preserve a balance of power in Northeast Asia. We cannot expect, of course, that China will approve of every detail of American strategy in the region. But China should endorse the basic features of the American posture: the gradual development of Japan's Self-Defense Forces in ways that do not threaten the security of Tokyo's neighbors, the maintenance of the Japanese-American Mutual Security Treaty, closer coordination between American and Japanese forces, and the preservation of an effective American base structure in Northeast Asia.

China and the United States also have significant common interests on the Korean peninsula. Both countries are opposed to either the resumption of conventional hostilities along the DMZ or the use of terrorism by the North against the South. Both would like to see a resumption of dialogue between Pyongyang and Seoul, and hope that this will, over time, lead to a reduction of tensions and an expansion of economic and cultural contacts between the two Koreas. And both Beijing and Washington would prefer that North Korea maintain a close relationship with China, that it not fall exclusively into the Soviet orbit, and that it eventually adopt a program of reform and liberalization similar to that undertaken by the PRC in the post-Mao period.

Despite these important similarities, however, the fact remains that China and the United States are committed by formal alliance to different parties on the Korean peninsula. This limits their flexibility in dealing with the Korean question and, in the extreme case, sustains the remote possibility of conflict between them should war break out in Korea once again.

In light of these considerations, the United States should express its appreciation to Beijing for its present policies toward Korea. We should urge China to continue its efforts to develop its own unofficial relations with South Korea, to dissuade Pyongyang from using force against the South, and to encourage North Korea to reform its economy and expand its commercial relations with the rest of the world. Washington should also seek China's understanding—if not its open support—for the American alliance with Seoul, the stationing of American military forces in South Korea, and regular military exercises between American and South Korean forces. Still, we must recognize that Beijing's leverage is limited. We cannot expect China to guarantee peace on the Korean peninsula or to compel change in North Korea's internal political and economic systems. We must also recognize that Beijing's ties with Pyongyang and its desire to prevent a North Korean realignment with the Soviet Union will hamper the establishment of official relations, particularly in the diplomatic realm, between China and South Korea.

If it is to be sustained and expanded, China's growing relationship with South Korea should be balanced, to a degree, by a gradual increase in American ties with North Korea. It is appropriate to begin with unofficial and informal scholarly exchanges and to move on to economic relations and formal diplomatic contacts only if there is progress in the dialogue between the two Koreas. In the early stage of this process, it is completely appropriate for the United States to ask Beijing, if it is willing, to serve as an intermediary, in order not only to open communication with Pyongyang but also to increase North Korea's stake in its relationship with China.

As Beijing adopts a more independent policy in the strategic arena, the relationship between China and the United States will become increasingly rooted in the economic ties between the two countries. Indeed, the evolution of Sino-American relations since 1984 has raised issues of trade and investment to the top of their bilateral agenda in recent years.

Both nations have a strong interest in the expansion of their economic relationship. For China, America is an important source of technology, capital, and markets, which can be of considerable assistance to the PRC's development program. Furthermore, the structure and operation of the American economy and the regulatory policies employed by various levels of the U.S. government can provide Beijing with much useful information, both positive and negative, as Chinese leaders grapple with the problems of economic reform. This is not to say that the United States will dominate China's foreign economic relations, that Beijing will mechanically copy the political or economic system of the United States, or that the Chinese will adopt American ideological concepts or philosophical values. China can be predicted to forge economic relations with as many nations as possible and to retain distinctively Chinese and socialist characteristics in the course of its development and reform. But the economic and cultural relationship with the United States will remain a significant component in China's drive for modernization.

Economic cooperation with China has many advantages for the United States as well. There is, first of all, the potential for profit in China. The United States has a comparative advantage in several sectors in which Chinese planners are especially interested, including energy extraction, transportation, communications, electronics, and agricultural technology. Great potential for increasing American exports to China exists in all these areas. In addition, as the investment climate in China improves, there may be further opportunities for American firms to establish manufacturing facilities in China, with the output sold either on the Chinese domestic market or to consumers in third countries.

Moreover, the economic relationship with China has certain prospective strategic benefits for the United States. Admittedly, there can be no absolute guarantee that a successfully modernizing China will employ its growing economic and military resources in ways that are fully congruent with American interests. But a China whose program of development and reform is reasonably successful and a China that has acquired a stake in a mutually beneficial economic and scientific relationship with the United States and with other friendly Asian nations is more likely to continue to promote stability and prosperity in the Asia-Pacific region than a China whose efforts at modernization have failed or whose attempts to participate in the world economy have been rebuffed. Conversely, were the United States to take a skeptical or aloof attitude toward China's economic modernization, such a posture would not prevent China's development, but instead would virtually ensure that Beijing would adopt a hostile stand toward the United States and its allies in Asia.

Although China and the United States can benefit from extensive economic interaction, the remaining dissimilarities in economic structure, philosophy, and interest will inevitably introduce some tensions into their commercial relationship. The Chinese can be expected to object to the rise of protectionism in the United States and will criticize the remaining restrictions on the export of advanced Western technology to China—both those administered by the American government and those implemented by COCOM.[16] Americans, in turn, will protest the extent to which the Chinese market remains closed to foreign imports and point out the ways in which the Chinese investment climate falls short of the ideal. A continuing dialogue between the two societies, involving the business and academic communities as well as their respective governments, will be necessary to identify these problems at an early stage and to develop effective and feasible solutions.

Although the common strategic and economic interests of the two countries serve to promote a stable and friendly relationship between the United States and China, their differences over Taiwan remain a latent irritant to Sino-American ties. The two nations share a common interest in preventing the Taiwan question from complicating their relations. Nonetheless, the continuing American interest in a peaceful future for Taiwan—an interest that Washington has consistently reiterated since the Shanghai Communiqué of 1972—potentially contradicts the Chinese insistence that the Taiwan question is a domestic matter in which no foreign power has the right to interfere.

As Chinese analysts learn more about the situation on Taiwan and come to a better understanding of American attitudes toward the issue, there is reason for optimism that the leadership in Beijing will adopt a more patient and flexible position on this sensitive subject. Even so, were the United States to appear to renege on any of its prior commitments to Beijing on the Taiwan question, whether by attempting to reestablish official relations with Taipei, by increasing the sale of arms to the island, or by abandoning its acknowledgment of Beijing's position that Taiwan is part of China, the Taiwan issue could easily be reignited, and Sino-American relations could enter a period of renewed discord. Similarly, the emergence of a powerful movement for Taiwanese independence would also complicate American relations with China.

At present, three aspects of American policy toward Taiwan

[16]COCOM is the abbreviation for the Paris-based Coordinating Committee—consisting of the NATO countries plus Japan and minus Iceland—which oversees the export of strategic goods to Communist countries.

deserve particularly careful consideration. One is the sale of American military equipment and arms to the island. The provision of a limited quantity of defensive weapons and production technology to Taiwan serves as an appropriate symbol of the continuing American interest in a peaceful future for the island, increases Taipei's self-confidence in dealing with Beijing, and improves Taiwan's ability to defend itself in the unlikely event that China should decide to use force against it.

At the same time, Taiwan's security depends as much on political factors as on the military balance in the Taiwan Straits. In the communiqué issued by Beijing and Washington in August 1982, the United States stipulated that it would gradually reduce the quantity of arms sold to Taiwan and would not improve the quality of equipment above that provided at the time of the normalization of Sino-American relations. If American arms sales were to violate the limits established by the agreement, the resulting deterioration of Sino-American relations would reduce Beijing's stake in preserving peace in the Taiwan Straits. Paradoxically, therefore, an excessive level of American arms transfers to Taiwan, although intended to enhance the island's security, might actually serve to endanger it.

A second area of concern is the American attitude toward the ultimate solution to the Taiwan question. Beijing's leaders often say that they would like the United States to "promote" the reunification of Taiwan and the mainland, explaining that they wish Washington would facilitate unofficial contact across the Taiwan Straits, encourage negotiations between Taiwan and the PRC, or endorse Beijing's formula of "one country, two systems." In response to these requests, the United States should indeed make clear that it has no interest in preserving the separation of Taiwan from the mainland and no objection whatsoever to the reunification of China, as long as it occurs through a peaceful and mutually acceptable process of convergence and dialogue. Moreover, the United States is already serving as a neutral arena in which intellectuals from Taiwan and the mainland meet on an increasingly frequent and regular basis to discuss problems of common interest. Their dialogue has already helped those on both sides of the Taiwan Straits to acquire more realistic, informed, and flexible images of one another. As Secretary of State George Shultz said in an important statement in Shanghai in March 1987, the United States supports a "continuing evolutionary process toward a peaceful resolution of the Taiwan question," and "welcome[s] developments, including indirect trade and increasing human interchange, which have contributed to a relaxation of the tensions in the Taiwan Straits."[17]

On the other hand, the United States is well served by its further position, stated as early as the Shanghai Communiqué of 1972, that the Taiwan question should ultimately be settled "by the Chinese themselves." Foreign involvement—and particularly American involvement—is not the key to the resolution of the Taiwan issue. Rather, the solution depends on development in all three parts of China itself: continued stability, prosperity, and liberalization on the mainland to reduce the gap between its political and economic system and that of Taiwan; further progress toward creating a more democratic and representative government on Taiwan, which can more confidently and effectively forge its own contacts with Beijing; and effective implementation of the Sino-British agreement on the future of Hong Kong, to build confidence in the viability of the formula of "one country, two systems." It would be unwise and unnecessary for the United States to serve as a mediator between the two parties, to attempt to sponsor formal negotiations between them, or to endorse or reject either side's negotiating position. Indeed, by reintroducing a potentially devisive issue into American domestic politics, any of these steps could well be counterproductive.

Third, the United States will also have to consider its response to the growing calls from opposition leaders in Taipei for the "self-determination" of Taiwan. Much depends on the precise meaning of this deliberately ambiguous term. The United States need have no reservations about the desirability of restructuring the political system in Taiwan so as to take the wishes of the people of the island into fuller account, or of giving Taiwan's representatives their rightful role in shaping the island's future relationship with the mainland. Both are logical implications of the broader American interest in political liberalization throughout Asia and of the principle that the future of Taiwan should be settled peacefully by the Chinese themselves. On the other hand, it would be undesirable for the United States to endorse a unilateral declaration of independence by any government or movement on the island. Instead, we should point out that only a formula that is mutually acceptable to both Taipei and Beijing can offer an enduring and viable resolution of the Taiwan question.

Unlike Great Britain or China, the United States is not directly involved in the future of Hong Kong. Nonetheless, we share with both Beijing and London an interest in the prosperity and stability of Hong Kong both before and after 1997. Accordingly, we join them in

[17]*Department of State Bulletin* 87:2122 (May 1987), pp. 10-11.

75

hoping that the agreement providing for the eventual return of Hong Kong to Chinese sovereignty will be implemented smoothly and effectively.

In pursuit of this interest, the United States should reinforce the arguments currently being made by the British government, the local administration in Hong Kong, and influential citizens in the territory that some degree of political reform and liberalization, and the insititution of effective legal guarantees against unwarranted encroachments on Hong Kong's autonomy, will be necessary if the residents of Hong Kong are to retain confidence in their system of governance after 1997. Such a position should, however, acknowledge and welcome the flexibility and restraint that, in most respects, the Chinese have shown on the Hong Kong question thus far.

Given its interest in the continued prosperity of Hong Kong, the United States has a further responsibility to help forge the institutional arrangements that will be required if Hong Kong is to enjoy the same standing in the international economic order as a special administrative region of China that it does today. Some of these steps will concern bilateral questions, such as recognizing the new travel documents issued by the Hong Kong government, renegotiating aviation agreements with the territory, and the like. Others will involve facilitating Hong Kong's participation, in its new status, in the major institutions of the international economy, from the Asian Development Bank to the General Agreement on Tariffs and Trade. Steady progress along both these dimensions, well in advance of 1997, will help bolster Hong Kong's confidence in the viability of its future status.

The combination of common interests and differing perspectives that emerges from this review of Chinese and American policies toward Northeast Asia has important implications for Sino-American relations. The commonalities make it highly unlikely that China and the United States will ever again become adversaries, as they were in the 1950s and 1960s. At the same time, however, the differences in outlook between the two countries, together with Beijing's desire to preserve its independence in international affairs, will prevent China from seeking a decisive and permanent alignment with the United States against the Soviet Union, as seemed to be its intention in the mid-1970s.

This implies that Americans must come to accept a somewhat ambiguous relationship with the PRC—a relationship in which there are points of divergence as well as convergence in the policies of Beijing and Washington. If we no longer need fear a Sino-Soviet alliance, as in the 1950s, neither can we hope for a "China card" to play against the Soviet Union, as was the hope in some quarters in the 1970s. Understanding such a relationship may well be difficult for Americans, who feel more comfortable in situations in which the line between friend and foe is more clearly drawn. Still, comprehending and accepting the complex character of Sino-American ties will be the key to building a stable and sustainable relationship with the PRC.

Implications for Japanese-American Relations

Given the centrality of Japan in American policy toward Northeast Asia, it is appropriate to conclude this study with a special focus on the implications of the new era in Chinese foreign policy for Japanese-American relations.

Viewed from a broad historical perspective, the triangular relationship between Japan, China, and the United States has been highly unstable, due primarily to the traditional rivalry between China and Japan. Japanese intervention in China—from the demands for political and economic privileges in the 1910s to the all-out invasion in the late 1930s—was one of the principal causes of war between the United States and Japan in the 1940s. In the 1950s and 1960s, even though the Japanese-American alliance was firmly in place, there remained a noticeable tension between the Japanese desire to trade with China and the American insistence on an embargo of the PRC. Then, when the United States launched its historic rapprochement with China in the early 1970s, Washington's failure to consult with Tokyo before dispatching Henry Kissinger on his secret visit to Beijing created widespread shock, irritation, and bewilderment in Japan.

When China and the United States established formal diplomatic relations at the end of 1978, the Carter administration pointed out that, for the first time in nearly a century, there were prospects for friendly relations among the United States, Japan, and China. No longer would the United States have to choose between Beijing and Tokyo. Nor would Japan have to choose between its relations with the United States and its ties with China. This provided additional assurances for stability in the relations among three of the major powers in East Asia and thus for peace and stability in the region as a whole.

This analysis contains an important truth. The United States and Japan today do have common interests with regard to China. Both Tokyo and Washington want to maintain friendly, stable, and beneficial relations with Beijing. Both want China to continue to serve as a force for stability and prosperity in Northeast Asia. Both Japan and the United States therefore share an interest in supporting China's current program of modernization, and both hope that the present economic and political reforms undertaken under Deng Xiaoping will continue and succeed.

Likewise, the United States and China also have common interests with regard to Japan. Both support Tokyo's claim to the Northern Territories, the four small islands off the coast of Hokkaido that have been occupied by the Soviet Union since the end of World War II. Both agree on the value of the Japanese-American security relationship, not only as a counterweight to Soviet expansion in Northeast Asia, but also as a way of obviating the need for Japan to develop a large defense establishment, possibly including nuclear weapons, of its own. Both benefit from their economic relationship with Japan, but voice similar complaints about the cultural, structural, and macroeconomic factors that restrict their access to the Japanese market.

Despite these significant common interests, there remain noticeable differences in perspective among the three countries. Compared with Americans, Japanese often are more pessimistic about the prospects for Chinese modernization and more cautious about the consequences should it succeed. They are more likely to point to the obstacles that work against economic development in the PRC and to warn about the possible consequences should Beijing develop powerful military forces. Many Japanese appear to favor independence for Taiwan, and yet they are reluctant to see their country become actively involved in the Taiwan question. And, of course, Japan and the United States see each other as competitors for the Chinese market for imported technology and equipment.

A comparison of Chinese and American attitudes toward Japan also reveals some potentially significant differences, particularly on military questions. Almost alone among Asia-Pacific actors, most Americans see Japan as an overly pacifist nation, reluctant to assume a fair share of the burden for its own security. China, like most other countries in the area, perceives Japan as a highly nationalist and chauvinist society, in which the resurgence of militarism remains a genuine possibility. As a result, American officials are more likely than their counterparts in China to support increases in Japanese military spending and an expansion of Japan's responsibility for its own defense.

The resulting differences in policy require closer consultation and dialogue among the three countries than has been the case in the past. China should not be allowed to become, as it was in the 1930s, a major cause of conflict in U.S.–Japan relations, nor even, as it was in the early 1970s, a source of shock and dismay for either party. Nor should Japan be permitted to become a major irritant in American relations with China. In this regard, three issues bear careful consideration.

First, given the remaining concerns in Tokyo about a strong China, a program of strategic cooperation between China and the United States warrants careful consultation between Tokyo and Washington on its pace and content. Although Japan cannot be given a veto over American relations with the PRC, it is necessary that the military relationship between China and the United States be designed with Japanese interests in mind. Japan would understandably be particularly displeased to see the United States assist in the rapid development of China's projective military capability, particularly its naval forces.

Conversely, the United States should understand that a rapid expansion of the Japanese armed forces would produce considerable alarm in China. Moreover, to the extent that this is seen as the result of American pressure and is regarded as evidence that the United States is not adequately taking into account Chinese interests in formulating its policy toward Japanese rearmament, such a development could also do damage to American relations with Beijing. Already, Chinese analysts privately ask their American colleagues whether the United States has carefully considered the longer-term consequences of its encouragement of increases in the Japanese military budget. As noted above, the United States should seek to reassure China that the Japan of today is very different from the Japan of the 1930s and that contemporary Asia has also changed markedly over the last 50 years. The resurgence of Japanese militarism should not, therefore, be regarded as especially probable, particularly given the growing interdependence of the Japanese and American economies. Nevertheless, China does deserve to be fully informed by both Tokyo and Washington about plans for Japanese military modernization and Japanese-American strategic cooperation so that the apprehensions and misunderstandings in Beijing can be reduced to a minimum.

Second, Tokyo and Washington need also to discuss their involvement in China's modernization effort. To a degree, the two countries can cooperate in encouraging China to improve its investment climate so as to attract more foreign capital. Such a collective effort would be in the interest of all three countries. But there are other issues related to China's modernization that may prove more controversial. In particular, the United States will find it difficult to accept a situation in which China attempts to build trade surpluses with the United States in order to finance a chronic trade deficit with Japan. Equally, the United States would object if a disproportionate amount of the capital that China drew from the World Bank—which, in turn, comes largely from American sources—were used for the import of Japanese technology. There is also a need for a common policy on the export of advanced technology to China—the development of which will require consultations with Europe as well as with Japan.

Finally, the Taiwan issue is also a possible irritant in the triangular relationship between the three countries. Japan shares the American interest in a peaceful future for the island but has thus far been reluctant to explain its perspective to Beijing. Instead, Tokyo gives the impression that it would like the United States to bear all the risks and costs of pursuing this common interest. Such an attitude is increasingly difficult for the United States to understand. Just as Japan is gradually assuming its share of the military burden in defending its home territory, so too it must shoulder part of the political burden of promoting its interests abroad.

At the same time, an overly aggressive or insensitive Japanese approach toward Taiwan could lead to a deterioration of Sino-Japanese relations, as has already occurred in 1987. If this development were to continue, Chinese suspicions about American intentions concerning the island could concomitantly be heightened. If it is in the American interest that Japan should take a more active role in promoting a peaceful future for Taiwan, it is also in our interest that Taiwan be prevented from becoming a significant obstacle to the smooth development of Sino-Japanese relations.

The discussion of these three issues is not meant to imply that relations with China are a major problem in Japanese-American ties, for such is not the case. But the divergences in perception and policy among the three countries could threaten the long-term stability of their mutual relationships if they are not carefully monitored and addressed.

Suggested Reading

Barnett, A. Doak, *The Making of Foreign Policy in China: Structure and Process* (Boulder: Westview Press, 1985).

Ching, Frank, *Hong Kong and China: For Better or For Worse* (New York: The China Council of The Asia Society and the Foreign Policy Association, 1985).

Clough, Ralph N., *Embattled Korea: The Rivalry for International Support* (Boulder: Westview Press, 1987).

Harding, Harry, ed., *China's Foreign Relations in the 1980s* (New Haven: Yale University Press, 1984).

Harding, Harry, *China's Second Revolution: Reform After Mao* (Washington: The Brookings Institution, 1987).

Huan, Guo-cang, *Sino-Soviet Relations to the Year 2000: Implications for U.S. Interests* (Washington: The Atlantic Council, 1986).

Johnson, U. Alexis, George R. Packard, and Alfred D. Wilhelm, Jr., eds., *China Policy for the Next Decade* (Boston: Oelgeschlager, Gunn and Hain, 1984).

Kim, Samuel S., ed., *China and the World: Chinese Foreign Policy in the Post-Mao Era* (Boulder: Westview Press, 1985).

Lasater, Martin L., *The Taiwan Issue in Sino-American Strategic Relations* (Boulder: Westview Press, 1984).

Lee, Chae-jin, *China and Japan: New Economic Diplomacy* (Stanford: Hoover Institution Press, 1984).

Segal, Gerald, *Sino-Soviet Relations After Mao*, Adelphi Paper No. 202 (London: International Institute for Strategic Studies, 1985).

Sutter, Robert G., *Chinese Foreign Policy: Developments After Mao* (New York: Praeger, 1985).

About the Author

Harry Harding is a senior fellow in the Foreign Policy Studies Program at the Brookings Institution in Washington, D.C. He received his undergraduate education at Princeton and his graduate training at Stanford. He taught for a year at Swarthmore and for twelve years at Stanford before joining the Brookings staff in the fall of 1983. He is the editor of *China's Foreign Relations in the 1980s* (1984), which was sponsored by the China Council of The Asia Society. He is also the author of *Organizing China: The Problem of Bureaucracy, 1949-1976* (1981) and *China's Second Revolution: Reform After Mao* (1987), as well as many other works on Chinese domestic politics, foreign policy, and U.S.–China relations.

TE D